# Mother Dearest, Imperfect Love

# Mother Dearest, Imperfect Love

## A True Story

### Myrtle Morrison

Copyright © 2011 by Myrtle Morrison.

| Library of Congress Control Number: | | 2011903519 |
|---|---|---|
| ISBN: | Hardcover | 978-1-4568-8073-6 |
| | Softcover | 978-1-4568-8072-9 |
| | Ebook | 978-1-4568-8074-3 |

All rights reserved. No part of this book may be reproduced or transmitted in any form or by any means, electronic or mechanical, including photocopying, recording, or by any information storage and retrieval system, without permission in writing from the copyright owner.

This book was printed in the United States of America.

If you have bought this book without a cover, you should be aware that this book is stolen property. It was reported as "unsold and destroyed" to the publisher, and the author/ publisher have not received any payment for this "stripped" book.

This is to inform the readers that most of the names have been changed to protect the identity of individual in this book.

**To order additional copies of this book, contact:**
Xlibris Corporation
1-888-795-4274
www.Xlibris.com
Orders@Xlibris.com
92248

## Dedication

*I dedicate this book to my three children  
Allicia, Latisha and Tevin.  
My grandmother Alice (Momma),  
Aunt Icema & Uncle Beb.*

## Acknowledgements

To Vivian (Terry) Terrelonge: For all your dedication and support over the years and for all you have done to make this book a reality; I thank you from the bottom of my heart.

My brother Dane and his family, you have been a source of inspiration.

To Prudence, William, Pat and Oswald: Thanks for your constant encouragement. Sandra, you've always had faith in me.

Daniela, your advice and friendship kept me going. Kim, thanks for being there for me. Please know I am always here for you too.

Thanks to all those who wished me well in accomplishing my dream of writing this book.

# Prologue

All my life I have suffered in silence. All my life I have swallowed my pain, holding it inside my heart, hiding it behind my smiles. Over the years the hurt has become a part of my life, a part of my soul, a part of me, but I refused to let it continue.

It is time for me to open these arms of mine that clutch this pain so close to my chest. It is like a baby whom I have sheltered in my bosom all these years. But now I must let it go free. Before, I could not talk about these things without crying but now I'm adjusting. I've been writing down my thoughts. It is still painful to do this and it still makes me cry, but not as much as it used to. I have reached the point in my life where I feel I must express myself so I can heal. I need to heal and I must. Only then can I live.

There was a time when I felt that all I endured in my life was something to hide from the world forever. I was afraid and, at one time, I felt that I could not talk about it. I wanted to, but I was too ashamed. In the story of my life there are some things that made me cringe when I remembered them. Sometimes I thought about how I would feel if my life were an open book, fearing the judgment of others. But then I decided that I needed to write about my life, because my fears, pain and sorrows it's been bottled up for too long—much too long.

One day, instead of sinking back into my misery, I began to open up and speak of my pain. Like a tightly coiled rosebud that slowly opens to receive the warmth of the sun the tension in my heart began to ease, and the hurt, to dissolve.

Amidst the tears, I began to share my pain. As a child, I could not. As a young woman, I would not. The fear and the hurt were too strong. But now I am no longer afraid. No one can raise a hand to strike me. No one can stifle my truth.

By sharing my story, I hope to find healing and peace.

# Early Life In Jamaica

# 1

*Are you my mother?*

Clutching my grandmother's flowery cotton dress, I peeped around her hips to stare at the lady, light-skinned and beautiful, sitting there in our tiny living room. She had a small face and very black, straight hair that fell to her shoulders. She stared back at me and I ducked behind Momma, safe in the roundness of my grandmother's hip, hidden in the fullness of her long skirt. I said nothing, no words passed my lips; I was wishing for the mother I'd dreamed of for so long. But still, I was scared.

"Go to your mother, child." Momma's voice was kind but firm. She gave me a little nudge with her hip, trying to dislodge me from her garment. I clung to her, afraid to move from the safety of her shadow.

It was 1964, and I was seven years old a big girl, Momma would sometimes say, at that time I did not feel so big. I did not want to leave my grandmother's side, to walk across the room to the beautiful brown woman who sat at our dining table, watching me.

"Come here Blossom," I remember the woman saying. This time there was a little smile as she sat there with a bowl in front of her. It had some bright yellow things floating in milk. I did not know what they were, but it looked like some kind of baby food. I looked at the bowl then to the lady. She dipped the spoon into the bowl and held it out.

"Come to me," she said.

I wanted to go to her. With all my heart I wanted to step boldly towards her, let her take me in her arms, let her be the mother I always wanted. But my legs were frozen where they stood. This was my mother and she was a stranger to me I was afraid of strangers.

"Blossom, come here."

As I recall, the voice got sharper; and I could see that this woman who, was my mother, did not like it that I was not going to her. Her brows gathered in a frown and her lips tightened.

"Go, Blossom, my grandmother said, giving me a gentle shove. I had to move or tip over. Propelled by Momma's push, I took three quick steps then another slower one. Then finally I was standing at the table, right across from my mother, looking at her up close for the first time I could remember. I could see the soft powder on her face and the gloss on her lips. *Where were you all this time, my mother?*

A spoon full of the yellow flaky stuff was shoved at me, breaking into my thoughts.

"Here Eat this."

I stared at the spoon then at my mother. I shook my head and said no.

"Eat," she frowned again.

My legs began to tremble. I could not move due to the fear I had of this stranger who was my mother.

My mother then put the spoon to her mouth and began to chew. Within seconds, she put her hand to her lips, and the chewed-up flakes that disappeared into her mouth were back out into her fingers.

Before I knew what was happening, she was grasping my arm, pulling me towards her, pushing the flakes past my lips and into my mouth. I pulled back in horror and disgust, but I could not stop her chewed up yellow mess from, filling my mouth.

My stomach heaved as I gagged. A stream of vomit gushed out of my mouth with my dinner from the night before splashing the edge of the dining table and all over the floor. The woman shrieked. My grandmother must have dashed forward because I suddenly felt her holding me, her warm hands on my shaking shoulders—her strength the only thing keeping me from falling.

"Leave her alone," Momma said. "Just leave her alone."

I recall trembling, my fear and my disgust. I still remember this meeting. It is so fixed in my mind. It is my first real memory of my mother.

## 11

According to what I heard, my mother, Imogene Allen, left the sleepy district of Marlborough in the parish of Saint Elizabeth at the age of sixteen, and headed to Jamaica's capital city to seek her fortune. There in Kingston, she stayed with her eldest sister Winnie, who had moved to the city some years earlier and was operating a successful restaurant business. She was the most successful of Momma's thirteen children and commanded a great deal of respect from her siblings. While my mother lived with Winnie, she was given the responsibility of acting as a courier. She was accountable for transporting produce from the country to Kingston for the restaurant, and taking groceries and money from the city back to the family in the country.

It was later found out by my grandmother that on those trips to the country, she formed a liaison with a young man from the community named John. In Kingston, she also had a friendship with a young man named Aris—a fireman who had once professed interest in Winnie. Aris spent many off-duty hours at the restaurant. As a single man, many of his meals were eaten right there. He became a regular, even helping out in the restaurant from time to time. When Imogene got pregnant at eighteen, she refused to tell my grandmother who the father of her baby was. There was speculation that it had to be one of these two men. Whoever it was, Momma never knew for sure. But when it was time for registration, my mother gave me the name of the fireman.

As a Christian, my grandmother disapproved of Imogene's pregnancy out of wedlock. The relationship between the two women was turbulent. I was told by my grandmother that Dearest, as my mother was called by the family, was never contrite about her pregnancy. On the contrary, she was bold and abrasive as if she had the right to do as she pleased. She did not have the means to support herself, but that did not seem to matter.

On March 24, 1957, I was born. My mother named me Myrtle Adalsa Morrison. As a child growing up, and even into adulthood, I would often wonder why my mother gave me such a strange name. To me, the name was an indication that my mother had not cared enough to find a beautiful name for me—her first born.

Dearest stayed with me three months in Momma's house, during which time she continued to be disrespectful. Things finally came to a halt after my mother and my grandmother had another quarrel. "This cannot work," Momma argued. To be under her roof with a baby was one thing, but to be disrespectful on top of it, that was another.

"Dearest, you think you are a big woman now," Momma said. "But it's either you take the baby and go, or you leave the baby and go. But I am not going to put up with your bad behavior in this house."

So my mother left. In June 1957, when I was only three months old, she went back to Kingston, leaving me behind with my grandmother in Marlborough. Momma was left to be my guardian and caretaker. She told me that, at the time, my body was covered in so many rashes that she had to hold me on a pillow. However, with her tender love and care, I gradually healed.

As I grew, Momma became the mother I never had. My grandmother had raised thirteen children of her own, eight girls and five boys. And now, in her mature years, she had to raise me. In the house lived Uncle Beb, Uncle Vincent and Cousin Berris. Not far away lived Aunt Joyce, who was a great help to Momma back then. She had a hand in raising me, often making little dresses, braiding my hair and made sure I was taken care of in the absence of Momma.

Of all the relatives, I was closest to my grandmother. I would travel with her to the city during the summer holidays when she would visit her children. I can remember Momma pointing to a lady during one of our visits. "That's your mother," she said. I looked at the woman as I clung to Momma's hand, but all she did was stare back at me. She did not come over to touch me or to give me a hug. This woman, who stood watching me with a serious look on her face, was a total stranger to me.

As far as I was concerned, Momma was my mother and guardian she was always looking out for my well-being. She was the one who enrolled me in school. I was almost five and a half years old and had just started school when Jamaica became an independent nation. I remember Momma talking about Independence and I remember the teachers talking about it in school. There were celebrations in all 14 parish's and party's in all the schools welcoming Jamaica's independence. The British government gave cups and flag to schools all over Jamaica; we danced and celebrated by partying in the streets.

August 6, 1962, was a special day for all Jamaicans. For us, it was the birth of independence for Jamaican's. On that, our first Independence Day, we heard our national anthem for the first time. In school, we ceased from asking God to save our gracious queen and sang, "Eternal Father, bless our land." We were taught the new motto, "Out of many, one people". Jamaican's witnessed the red, white and blue Union Jack as it was lowered and in its place the black, green and gold Jamaican flag was raised on poles all over the island. Tiny black, green and gold flags were given to students all over the island.

Our Prime Minister, Sir Alexander Bustamante, gave an emotional speech to over twenty thousand people at the Jamaica National Stadium in Kingston. The message was to the entire nation as it was transmitted on the airwaves to even the humblest villages on the island. Fireworks lit up the skies in celebration of a new era for Jamaica.

The next day, all schools were closed and the day was declared a holiday. It was announced that our leaders would be holding the first session of Jamaica's parliament on that day. Princess Margaret, on behalf of the Queen, gave a speech in which, she congratulated and welcomed Jamaica as the newest member of the Commonwealth Family. Prime Minister Bustamante and the Leader of the Opposition, Norman Manley, both gave speeches in response, speaking of the people's new responsibility to create their own destiny and to build a safe and prosperous country.

During Independence Day, Momma brought home starlight and firecrackers for the older ones in the house, like Uncle Vincent, who was about sixteen. Vendors were selling the firecrackers at every corner for the celebrations. At church, the pastor spoke about Independence. Everyone was excited, and I remember that time as a joyful one.

Still, this did not make growing up in Marlborough easy. Sometimes things were tough with my grandmother—she was not always able to afford all that I needed. I remember the principal coming to my grandmother's house to tell her I had potential and possibly a bright future ahead of me. "You should send Myrtle to do extra lessons," he advised.

Momma was rich in spirit, but not so fortunate financially. She never had much money and raising me without any contributions from my mother made it worse. Everything fell on Momma's shoulders, so the opportunity to take those extra lessons passed me by.

Still, I am forever grateful to my grandmother. I never held it against her because what she lacked in wealth, she more than made up for in love. Some of my earliest memories include her sitting me on the trunk, which served as seat cum bed, gently spooning food into my mouth as I resisted. I was not a big eater, but Momma was patient. She always made sure I was well fed. The one thing she could afford was to give me was love—and she gave me lots of it.

I had always been a picky eater and wouldn't eat from anyone else. But with Momma, I would eat off her plate, drink from her cup and even re-chew the sugarcane husks she had taken out of her mouth as a way to feel close to her. She was both mother and father to me as I was growing up. I loved Momma so much that I clung to her constantly.

I had various challenges in life, one of them being unexpected changes when I was a student in elementary school, but Momma could not protect me from the rough transition. Like any other child, there were times when I enjoyed elementary school and other times when I wished I did not have to go. My school troubles were mainly because of a boy who made my life a living hell.

"Leopard," Bruce would whisper into the back of my neck. "Hey! you leopard." He sat at the desk right behind mine—the perfect vantage point so he could tease me without getting caught.

"Freckle-faced leopard," he whispered. Those in hearing distance would giggle and snicker, enjoying his wit and reveling in my shame. I couldn't do anything about it and the teacher never caught him. No, he was a master bully and I felt powerless. I had to endure his torment for three years at elementary school but the teasing and whispers in class were nothing compared to the harassment I faced at recess. He would lay in wait and, once I went outside, that was when he let loose.

"Leopard, leopard, freckle-faced leopard," he chanted. Everybody laughed and I would cried all alone and afraid.

The worst times were when he would wait for me after school, when he would throw rocks and shouting his favorite line: "Leopard, leopard, freckle-faced leopard."

And every day, as I ran home as fast as I could, I would curse my light brown skin and the chocolate brown spots spattered all over my face. So many days I wondered what I would look like without those spots. I rubbed bushes on them, trying to get them to disappear, but to no avail. I could not change my skin. I could only try to stay as far away from Bruce as I could.

Another name they used to call me at school was "dry land tourist". Although I was from rural Saint Elizabeth, I did not speak deep Patois—the local dialect that most of the children in the country spoke. Momma never allows it.

"Speak properly!" She'd reprimanded me if she heard me speaking Patois. "It is not 'whe' you a go?' It is 'where are you going?'."

Because of this upbringing, I always sounded a little different from my classmates; and they never stopped teasing me for it. But it was not just my speech that made me seem different—Momma also taught me to carry myself like a lady. And so I was careful to walk to school in a lady liked fashion with my head high as if I was balancing a book on head, in my neatly pressed navy blue school uniform and crisp white blouse.

Another person in my life who insisted on proper grammar was my sixth grade teacher, Miss Vie. I loved Miss Vie, partly because her children and I were friends. She was also a great role model to me. She was a very good teacher in English and Math and professional in everything she did. She was also a strict disciplinarian, but it did not bother me because I did not misbehave in class.

However, one day her strictness worked against me. Miss Vie was in the middle of teaching the lesson when I felt like I needed to go to the bathroom really badly, I felt like my bladder was going to burst. I hesitated for a moment then went up to the teacher's desk. "Miss," I said, "please allow me outside."

Miss Vie put up two fingers, silencing me. "No," she scolded. "Go sit and do your work."

I hesitated, wanting to run to the bathroom, but I was scared. How could I defy my teacher? I shuffled back to my desk and sat down. Maybe I could hold it till the bell rang, I thought. I waited and I waited. I sat there, growing more and more uncomfortable by the minute, but still the bell did not ring. I bit my lip, I squeezed my legs together, but still the feeling would not go away. I gathered up my courage and walked back to the teacher's desk. "Miss Vie," I said, "please allow me to go outside."

"No," she said again, more firmly this time. "Go finish your work."

I went back to my seat, distressed. I needed to go so badly. I waited and waited until I could not stand it any longer. I felt ready to burst. I stood at my desk and raised my hand. "Miss Vie, please allow me outside," I urged.

This time when she looked at me she must have seen how close I was to wetting myself because she finally nodded and said, "Go."

But it was too late. I could not turn. I could not move. I stood there and the pee ran out of me, down my legs, into my socks and shoes, onto the floor. There was nothing I could do to stop it.

I wished I could disappear from that classroom. What would my friends think of me? I was nine years old, not a baby anymore. How could this be happening to me? Everybody would certainly laugh at me and never let me forget this most embarrassing day of my life. I kept my eyes down, refusing to look neither to the left nor to the right.

Mercifully, Miss Vie allowed me to go straight home. I dashed out of the classroom and did not look back. That evening my classmate, Richard, dropped off my books at my house and told me that he was the one they had made clean up my mess. I was too embarrassed to say anything. Thank goodness he wasn't laughing at me. I took the books and went back inside the house.

Next day, I dragged my feet as I walked to school. I didn't feel like looking ladylike. I did not feel like going to school at all, but Momma would never allow me to stay at home unless I was sick. I shuddered to think about the laughter I would have to face when I got to my class. And, as I expected, there was teasing. As usual, the ringleader was there. Still, by the end of the day, almost everyone seemed to have forgotten about the incident. Everyone except Bruce—He just did not know when to stop. It took days before he grew tired of the teasing. But much to my relief he became bored with it.

Through reflecting on this negative childhood, I have learned that people who bully others have negative beliefs about themselves. They suffer from low self-esteem, search for weakness in others and bully them in order to feel good about themselves. Behind close door bullies shake in fear. I taught my children to believe in themselves and not to let anyone treat them wrong. What felt like a curse during my childhood turned into a blessing that I will passed on to my children.

## 𝒯𝒯𝒯

My grandmother, Alice Rosan Taylor Allen, came from a place called Pike—a sleepy village in the northern region of the parish of Manchester. When she was very young, her family moved to Marlborough in the parish of Saint Elizabeth. There she lived with her parents and her sisters Lenora, Aminah, Susan, Lucy, Esther and her only brother; "One Son," as his parents named him.

Young Alice eventually had two children but remained unmarried until she met a short, light-skinned man by the name of Josiah. They fell in love, married and settled down together as a family. Soon, Alice bore children with Josiah—Lorenzo coming first, then Enos and then Winnie. Over the years they had other children: Bernice, Icema, Emma, Joyce, Imogene, Beb, Boyie and Vincent. Unfortunately, the two children she had prior to her marriage both passed away while still young, and their bodies were laid to rest on family land.

Alice married life was a turbulent one. It was not long after her union with Josiah that she found out that this handsome man she had married had a dark side to him. The man was a wife beater. He often turned violent, beating her and the children. She lived day, bearing the abuse that was the result of his temper

Then, as if the beatings were not enough, to her shock and dismay, Alice found out that her husband had other women, despite her devotion to him. Alice was stunned when she learned the identity of his mistress—her own sister, Lenora. Alice suffered in silence for years, devastated by the double betrayal. This was quite a blow to her, and it took several years before she was able to rise above the hurt, bury her anger and greet her sister with civility. By this time, Lenora had two children with Josiah: Eunice and Kevin. Over time, the wounds began to heal between the sisters. Eventually, Lenora felt comfortable enough to start visiting the home that Alice shared with Josiah.

Even with the passing of many years, Alice and her husband continued to quarrel frequently. She suffered both physical and emotional abuse at the hands of this man who had sworn to love and protect her. Temporary relief came several years later when Alice's children were teenagers—they were strong enough to protect their mother from the tyranny of Josiah's fists. Many times Lorenzo and Enos had to grab their father by the arms to hold him back, pinning him against the wall until he lost the energy to force through their constraint.

As the older children grew up and left home to seek a life for themselves, the younger ones were the only line of defense between Alice and her husband. She got no rest from his abuse until her husband was a mature man. Only then did he begin to slow down and mellow a bit. But his violent rage never left him.

Then one day, he fell ill. Within a short time, he died. And just like that, Momma found herself a widow. Fortunately most of her children were already grown and on their own. Still, this new way of life required some adjustment. But she was a determined woman and so she picked up the pieces of her life and moved on.

I was born the year following the death of my grandfather. In March 1957, my grandmother found herself busy with me, the new baby in the house and a new purpose in life. By the time Dearest left in June of that year, Momma had to become a full-time mother all over again.

The years went by and I grew healthy and strong with my grandmother's care. One day when I was eight years old, I heard Momma talking about a man who was coming to visit Jamaica. He was a minister and a big man in America, because he gave many speeches to the black people there, helping them to fight for their rights. Most people think Dr. Martin Luther King was a very brave man, and they admired the way he could give speeches that brought tears to your eyes and made you feel like joining his march for freedom and justice.

On June 20, 1965, Dr. Martin Luther King arrived in Jamaica along with his wife, Coretta. On the news, we heard that he would be delivering a sermon for the 1965 valedictory service for the University of the West Indies. He also gave a great speech at the National Stadium and everyone talked about how inspiring it was, especially the part where he said "if you are a street sweeper you should sweep the streets so well that you would be like the great artist painting his masterpiece." It made a lot of people feel good about themselves, about their work and about how their contributions to the country. Dr. Martin Luther King made us feel proud. Even though I was only eight, I saw how much the adults admired him—that made me admire him too.

That was why I was so sad when only three years later, in 1968, we heard that this great man had been killed. Momma was at home in Marlborough doing her gardening as usual when one of the neighbors rushed into the yard.

"Miss Alice, they killed him . . . Martin Luther King is dead."

Momma's jaw dropped as she stared at the bearer of this bad news. "What? They killed a good man like that?"

"Yes, the same one who came to Jamaica. I just heard and I ran down here to tell you. They shot him stone dead."

I could see the sorrow quickly spread across Momma's face. "Jesus have mercy upon them." She shook her head. "Jesus . . ." she sighed, "all these good people are getting killed."

That was one of the saddest days for Jamaica, even for the students in school. Some of the teachers even cried, I heard.

There was another great man who came to Jamaica who I can recall. When Haile Selassie visited Jamaica, Rastafarians acted like God himself had come. I could not understand the reason for all the excitement. The Emperor, as they called him, arrived on April 21, 1966. I turned nine just the month before, so I was sensible enough to know that this tiny man from Ethiopia could never be God. In church, we were told that God was a spirit and the only human form of God was His son, Jesus, I remember thinking.

How could Haile Selassie be God? As far as I was concerned, the Rastafarians had got it all wrong.

I heard when Selassie arrived at the airport he saw thousands of marijuana-smoking Rastafarians waiting for him. They had signs, praising him as the 'king of kings' and as 'God's anointed'. I guess he must have been scared, because he turned and went right back inside the aircraft. He only came back out after he had heavy security around him. I often wondered how the Rastafarians felt about that.

At around that time, my mother surprised Momma with a message sent to our local post office. Momma hurried into the yard—a telegram in her hand. It was a request for her to get twelve dozen jelly coconuts for my mother.

We got pen and paper to calculate exactly how many coconuts made up twelve dozen. We dug up an old exercise book that had a copy of the times tables.

"Twelve times twelve . . . one hundred and forty-four," Momma exclaimed. She then turned to me with a perplexed look on her face. "Why would Dearest want so many jelly coconuts?"

In the end Momma gathered as many coconuts as she could—it turned out to be fewer than a dozen. Soon after that, my mother sent another message to let Momma know that she was coming to the country.

I remember how excited we were upon hearing the news. We prepared for the visit, making sure the house was spotless. The floors gleamed after a good scrub with broad leaf bush. I swept up the leaves that had fallen from our numerous fruit trees and made sure that the outside of our house looked just as good as the inside. There I was, only nine years old, anxiously awaiting the arrival of this mother I barely knew. Still, I wanted to see her, to be close to her, to get a chance to be her daughter.

Then the day came for my mother, Dearest, to arrive. From early in the morning, each time we heard a car, Momma and I would run out to the front path to look. We could see the road almost a half mile away, but each time we ran out it was not her. Finally, there she came, looking small from afar, but then I noticed there was a tall man with her.

"It's them," I called out.

Momma and I ran down the pathway to meet them. My mother was smiling as she walked toward us—she looked truly happy.

I stood aside to let Momma and Aunt Dearest hug. I don't remember my mother hugging me. The man who had come with my mother kept smiling, but all I did was stare at him. He was a tall, light-skinned, Indian-looking man. He seemed pleasant, but I did not go near him. He was a stranger and I was afraid of strangers.

As I watched them, Aunt Dearest turned to look at the man, smiling with a twinkle in her eye. My heart stung when I noticed she only had eyes for him but noticed Momma smiling too—she was at ease as if she approved of him, whoever he was.

Aunt Dearest took her friend's hand and he held her as she walked. Her belly looked big, and I could guess she was going to have a baby. She seemed so excited and happy around him.

When I got to the house I watched from the window of the middle room as she showed him around the yard full of fruit trees. She was probably telling him which tree was hers. Momma had borne thirteen children and every one of them had been given a breadfruit tree on these two and a half acres of property.

After they left Momma could not stop talking about Aunt Dearest's new friend. "What a nice young man," she said. "That girl Dearest has been searching around so long. I'm so glad she found somebody nice. I just pray things work out for them."

I guess God answered Momma's prayer, because soon after the visit, Aunt Dearest invited Momma to her wedding. Momma and I journeyed to Kingston and stayed with one of her daughters. On the day of the wedding, we sat in the church, lost in a sea of strangers. I knew I had relatives there, but I stuck close to Momma—she was my security in this strange place. As I looked around, I noticed all the people there knew one another. They were smiling and talking, which made me realized they were not the strangers, I was.

Aunt Dearest was beautiful on her wedding day. Her full flowing dress covered her round belly, making her look broader and larger. The white veil on her head and the flowers in her hands made her look like a queen. She walked down the aisle to meet her groom and, on that summer day, they became husband and wife.

There's a lot I don't remember about that important day in my mother's life but now, as an adult with children of my own, I look back and I wonder how she could have left me out of her wedding. I still feel unwanted, thinking she treated me like a moment in her past she did not want included in her new one. When I looked at her wedding pictures, I was nowhere to be seen, even though I was her only child at the time. She did not ask me to be her flower girl; she did not even acknowledge my presence at her wedding. I was nothing but a stranger that day, especially to my own mother. I cannot help wondering what I could have done to this woman at such a tender age that she did not want me to be a part of her life.

# IV

Back in Marlborough, I went about my life as usual. I loved going to church with my grandmother. She would dress in her Sunday best and head out to church with me walking along beside her. Along the way, I practiced my 'ladylike' walk, holding my back straight, as I saw Momma doing, trying to be just like her. When we got to the church, she slid inside the pew and whispered prayers for a moment, then she shooed me off to the Sunday school program.

It was at Pond side Bethany Baptist Church that Momma would have the best time singing her Sankey song book and even getting into the spirit. When the spirit of the Lord came upon her, she would stand up and shout.

"Jesus," she cried. "My Lord, Jesus."

Then the panting would start then the hopping from one leg to the other, then the clapping of the hands. As a child her gyrates frightened me a little, as I grew older, I realized that this was what made my grandmother feel whole.

Momma had a favorite wig she wore to church. It had three thick plaits one at the front and one on each side. She tucked the ends of the plaits under her hat, so the thick hair framed her face. She was content going to church like that, until one day the pastor told her not to wear the wig anymore. Momma—disappointed he did not approve of her beloved wig—obeyed. The next Sunday she left it at home and only wore her hat.

One of Momma's church sisters, Miss Louise noticed right away. She stared at Momma, then said: "Sister Alice, how your face looks so, like when they singe rat?"

I could sense Momma's humiliation, but she did not respond. I was surprised she did not stand up for herself. Apparently, what Sister Louise said stayed in her mind—she eventually started wearing the wig again every-so-often until it became a regular part of her headgear again. So, even though her beloved Minister Powell had said, "Sister Alice, take off the wig", in her own quiet way, my grandmother asserted her right to feel confident and beautiful.

When I was about eleven year old, the deacon's son had a crush on me. He always wanted to hold my hand. Once he told me he loved me I rejected his tokens of affection, but inside I was happy that he liked me. Sometimes, when I would head for the bathroom with the girls, he would trail behind me and tug at my arm.

"Come here, Blossom," Aegon would whisper.

However, I shyly resisted. I secretly liked him too, but I did not want to tell him and I did not want him to embrace me around other people.

A few of my church friends knew we liked each other. Sometimes June, the pastor's daughter, whispered to me: "Aegon is outside." This filled me with excitement and, if I got the chance, I would dash outside and stand for a little with him by the side of the church and just talk. Even as I now look back, my memories of our puppy love still make me smile.

As a child, my greatest joy was to climb the fruit trees in the yard. Mangoes, avocados, oranges and apples—the trees were there for me to climb—and I could eat all the fruit I wanted. My district was the most beautiful place in the world to me. It was just a small town with one main road, where the houses were perhaps a few blocks apart. I loved Marlborough for its valleys and mountains, fruit trees and wild birds—it was so serene compared to Kingston. Best of all, it was just Momma and me in our humble rural paradise. By this time, Uncle Beb had gotten married and moved out to live with his wife. Uncle Vincent had moved to Kingston. Cousin Beres had gone to live with his father in the parish of Manchester.

But one day things changed. In the summer of 1969, my grandmother took me to the city to visit my aunts and uncles. Whenever Momma and I had to travel to Kingston, most times we walked to Balaclava—the nearest town—and board the train there. Other times we took a taxi to the train station. If we did the three-and-a-half mile trek on foot, we would always stop a few chains away from our destination and use a cloth to wipe the dust from our feet. At this point, we changed from our walking shoes to our dress shoes, ready for the train journey to the city.

It would take all day for us to travel from Balaclava to Kingston on the train. The diesel train was much faster, but the fare was a lot higher. We had to satisfy ourselves with taking the regular train, which went through several other towns, such as Comfort Hall,

Kendal, Porus and many more stops, which took several hours before it finally arrived in Kingston.

Each time the train passed through Kendal, I remembered the chilling story Momma told about the Kendal railway disaster, which was the second worst train wreck in the world up to that time. It took place on a Sunday, the first day of September in 1957—the same year I was born. Momma told me many people died that night. She became grief-stricken each time she spoke about it, as if she knew the people onboard. She often prayed for all those who died that disastrous night, as well as for the families affected.

According to the reports, the train was over crowded, with about a thousand, six hundred people, when there should have been fewer than one thousand. Hundreds of church people were on the train coming back from an excursion in Montego Bay. When the train got to Kendal, it picked up speed and derailed, killing almost two hundred people and injuring about seven hundred. The nation was thrown into deep mourning that September night.

Momma also told me ghost stories about the Kendal train crash. One of them was of a man who took a taxi to a house in Kingston. He got out of the car, telling the driver he was going inside to get the money to pay the fare. The taxi driver sat waiting in the car and, after a long while, the man still did not return. The driver then went up to the door and knocked. A woman answered. He told her he had just dropped off a man at this location and had been waiting for a long time for him to return with the fare. When the taxi driver described the person, the woman was astonished—the description was that of her husband who had died in the Kendal train disaster.

Each time the train stopped in Kendal, I felt a chill down my spine. I heard so much about that place, and about the deaths, that I could not help wondering if one day I would see a ghost. As we passed through Kendal, I would sometimes hear Momma whisper: "Lord, bless these people." I knew she was thinking about the people who died in there. Even though so many years had passed by, it seemed as if it was always fresh in her mind.

Back at our home, it was never a stale subject of conversation between her and my uncles. I believe the men in the family must have gone out to see the crash that night. Kendal was not far from Marlborough, so they must have journeyed there on foot. They had many stories to tell Momma. They talked about all the body parts scattered on the ground. These stories frightened me. I breathed a sigh of relief when the train pulled away from that station.

In Porus, vendors would come onto the train selling oranges, mangoes, apples, tangerines, peanuts and pepper shrimps. Whatever food items the passengers wanted, they could buy from these merchants—there was no need to leave the train. Momma would buy snacks for us to eat on our way.

On one of our journeys, I was about twelve years old; we were heading for Kingston to visit one of Momma's daughters in the Gordon Town community. On that train ride, I ate about two dozen pepper shrimp Momma bought at the stop in Porus. Momma knew how much I liked the pepper shrimp, so she bought me four packages, I ate so much that day that, by the time we got to Kingston, my bloated stomach started churning—I really needed a bathroom. I held it in, though, hoping I would be able to bear it until I got to my aunt's house.

When I got inside the bus heading for Papine, it was too much for me. "I need to go to the bathroom," I told Momma. "I can't hold it. I need to go now."

"Oh, my God," Momma said, surprised. She had no idea how badly I needed to go. "Take it easy, Blossom. Hold it, sweetheart—hold it."

I tried to hold it but it was there, right at the edge of my throat. Before I knew what was happening, vomit spewed out of my mouth and splashed all over the bus aisle. All the shrimp I consumed lay swimming in the pool of vomit.

Immediately, my urge to use the washroom disappeared. My stomach settled and I was fine. Since then, though, I have had a strong aversion to shrimp and I avoid it to this day. Each time I think of shrimp I remember that day.

I had a lot of aunts and uncles in Kingston, because Momma had so many children. She had no problem finding a place to stay when we were there. She would just go from one of children's place to another. She moved around so frequently that she never wore out her welcome.

On this trip, we were visiting Aunt Icema, when we were introduced to a little girl who came over to play. She stuck to my aunt and my grandmother who admired how bright she was. She could not have been more than four years old.

"What a sweet little thing," was Momma's reaction, and she asked Aunt Icema about the child.

"That's my neighbor's daughter," she told Momma. "She has five other children plus this one."

Later, Momma met the girl's mother and said in jest: "I want this one," while embracing the child under her arm.

"You can take her," the lady said.

Momma was stunned when the lady agreed to give up her daughter. Next day, Momma and Aunt Icema went next door again to hash out the details of the young girl who was coming to stay with us.

For the rest of our visit the girl continued to come over. She would never leave our side, as if she knew already we were her family. When it was time to head back to Marlborough, instead of it being a twosome, we were now a family of three. Still, Aunt Icema remained something of a guardian to Donna, even though Momma would be the one raising her.

It was fun initially having Donna's company at the house in Marlborough, but sometimes it was also a pain. The girl was a real tattletale. I could not do anything without her reporting it to my grandmother, which caused many arguments with Momma. Donna became somewhat of a wedge between us sometimes—and I hated that.

One thing we both enjoyed, however, was story time. In our house, we had no radio or television, but we did not miss those things at all. I was blessed with a grandmother who was a great storyteller. She told us lots of stories about Anancy, the trickster spider every night before going to bed.

One of my favorites was called '*My Father's Best Riding Horse*'. In that story, a very proud and handsome tiger, who loved to dress in his three-piece suit and top hat, paced back and forth through the town. Showing himself off to all the girls. Because Tiger was so handsome and strong, everybody admired him and no one would bother him on his walks. The only person who had no respect for Brer Tiger was Brer Anancy. Both of them had fallen in love with the same girl—the prettiest one in the district.

One day, Brer Anancy decided to get Brer Tiger out of the picture, so he told his beloved Serena that Brer Tiger was nothing more than his father's old time riding horse. Serena was disgusted that a former pack animal would dare to court her. So, the next time Brer Tiger came visiting, she chased him off her verandah. When he asked why, she told him the story she had heard from Brer Anancy.

In a rage, Brer Tiger went looking for Brer Anancy and found him lying in bed with a damp cloth on his head. He demanded that Brer Anancy go with him to Serena's house to admit his lie. Brer Anancy agreed, but said he was dying and was so weak that Brer Tiger would have to carry him. He said Brer Tiger would have to go down on all fours so he could hold on to him on the way to Serena's house. Brer Anancy did such a good job of faking his illness that Brer Tiger believed him. So, he took Brer Anancy on his back and raced to Serena's house so the confession could be made.

As they approached Serena, who was still standing on her verandah, Brer Anancy jammed his heels into Brer Tiger's side to make him run faster. He pulled out a whip and shouted; "See,

Serena! I told you Brer Tiger is nothing but my father's old riding horse!" He then jumped off and dashed away to safety. In shame, Brer Tiger ran off and was never seen again in the district.

Momma also told us stories about her children and about her husband who had died in 1956. We did not like the stories about her abusive husband, but the stories about her children were sometimes funny. Most of all, we loved the ghost stories.

Donna and I would sit with Momma in the main room that served as our living room, which had a double bed. There was a dining table pushed up against the wall, two chairs at the table and a couple of other wooden chairs in the corners. It was a cheerful room—Momma had cut out pictures from magazines and clippings from newspapers and pasted them all over the limestone. I never got tired of reading the articles plastered on our walls. In this front room, we would curl up on the floor at Momma's feet and she would tell us about ghosts and spirits—tales that sent us to bed shivering with fear.

The scariest ones were about the rolling calf. This was an evil spirit that had entered the body of a cow. Most times, it was the spirit of a butcher who had been wicked in his lifetime. The rolling calf had blood-red eyes, clanking chains, and fire coming from its nostrils. At night, it would look for travelers and chase them down the dark roads, snorting fire at them. To escape, one had to drop things along the road for the calf to count. Legend had it, this distracted the nasty cow. Another trick Momma told us about was to race to the next crossroad before it got there, open a penknife and stick it in the ground. Every time I heard these stories

I was glad I did not have to be out on the road alone at night.

These tales terrified us, but it did not stop Donna and me from asking for more. But one day we were blessed—or cursed—with a real life ghost story of our very own. It all began with a box of clothes.

"Where did all of this come from, Momma?"

I watched as my grandmother pulled out beautiful dresses, shoes, blouses and nightgowns from the box.

"Your Auntie from the States—they came from her house."

"You mean uncle Enos' wife the waitress? The one whose funeral you and uncle Beb went to at the Church in Siloah?"

Momma nodded, "but she had these before she was sick; these clothes are good."

I was happy that Momma had been given the box of clothes and was eager to try on some of them, even though they would be way too large for me.

Momma left me with the box and went out to check on the pot boiling on the wood fire. I immediately picked out a garment, a long pink housecoat, and decided to try it on. I slipped my arms into the sleeves and shrugged the coat onto my shoulders then I tied the sash. It was so long that it swept the floor, but I enjoyed the soft feel of the fabric against my skin.

I was twirling around, admiring the house coat, when I pushed my hands inside the pockets and came out with a wad of tissue all rolled up. I opened my fist and the tight wad loosened. That's when I saw it—the blood—dried blood filled the ball of tissue paper. Goosebumps covered my skin and I dropped the tissue onto the floor.

"Momma!" I yelled. "Momma, come look here!"

My yell must have startled her, because within seconds she was in the room with me.

"What's wrong, child?"

"Look." I pointed to the ball of paper on the floor. "There's blood on the tissue that was in this pocket."

Momma's eyes widened. Then she was reaching for me, pulling the sash, stripping the offending garment from my shoulders.

"Take it off, Blossom."

I quickly shed the robe and we both stood there for a time, staring at the ball of tissue in the middle of the floor. Finally, my grandmother moved. Gingerly, she bent and picked up the tissue. She went outside and threw it on the garbage heap. When she came back, she gathered up all the clothes—including the pink robe—and packed them back into the box the garments came from.

"It looks like this is the robe she was wearing in the hospital." Momma shook her head and her frown told me she was unhappy. "I can't believe Enos would let them send me the recent stuff she wore".

A few days passed; and eventually Momma and I forgot about the bloody tissue paper. My grandma went back to her digging and planting and her church, while I went back to going to school and climbing trees. Donna continued to be the pesky little chatterbox that she had always been.

Although Momma had packed the clothes away, there was something from Aunt Megan that she continued to use—long, sheer curtains now adorned our windows. Momma loved them, not only because they came from one of her most beloved daughters-in-law, but also because of the way they let the light in during the day. The rich cream color made the place look bright and cheerful. But at night, they were too sheer to afford us any privacy, so she would throw a red cotton cloth over the windows.

One morning when we woke up and came out of Momma's room, we found that something strange happened—the red cloths that had covered each of the three windows were now hanging off to the side.

I stood there, frozen, and could not keep my eyes of them.

"It looks like your Aunt Megan is doing her works inside this house," my grandmother said.

I felt the fine hairs on my body stand on end.

"Looks like she's vexed that we covered up her curtains," Momma continued. "But that's why I covered them with red, you know. I didn't think she would mess with red."

Still shaking her head, Momma walked over to the first window and took down the red covering. Immediately the morning sun began to shine through. Deep in thought, Momma folded the red cloth slowly and deliberately as she stared out the window.

I did not pay any more attention to the mystery that day. I had my chores to do, sweeping up the leaves under the trees, rubbing the floor with a coconut brush until it gleamed and helping Momma feed the chickens and the pigs. After that, I got to play with Donna. Although the little girl could be annoying, she was my only companion and playmate, so I let her tag along. We pulled up the grass and used the roots as hair, braiding it, as if we were braiding a doll's hair.

It was only when the orange sun began to fall behind the hills that Momma called us from the cow pasture, which was across from the house, to get ready for bed. It had been a busy day and we were exhausted, but not too exhausted to skip our baths. Momma would never have a couple of sweaty little girls in her bed. Donna and I raced for our washtubs. One thing we did not want was for the night to fall before we had our wash—it was too scary to be outside after dark.

Damp and clean, our nighties clinging to our shivering bodies. Donna and I leaned our washtubs against the big concrete tank and headed inside, as the soft blanket of dusk now falling around our shoulders. Donna gave a big yawn, while Momma lit the Home Sweet Home lamp. It was finally time for bed and time for our stories.

"Which story are you giving us tonight?" I asked. I was hoping Momma would say, she was going to tell us an Anancy story, then I would ask for the one where Anancy tricked Brer Rabbit and Snake and got them thrown off the train.

"I'm too tired tonight. You girls go to bed."

"But Momma, just one story?" I pleaded Donna's face showed her support.

"I have too much on my mind right now," she began.

Nevertheless, Donna and I had already sat down at her feet. We were not taking no for an answer.

That night we did get our Anancy story. Momma told us the one about Brer Anancy and Sister Peel-Head Fowl. Seeing the farmers passing along the road with their produce, Brer Anancy found a way to trick them into giving him all their food. He came up with a law, to which all agreed, that if anyone disrespected another, they had to give all their goods to the one who had been treated rudely. Then he set himself up on a huge boulder with a hoe. Each time a passing farmer asked what he was doing, he would say he was preparing the ground for planting. Of course, the farmer would laugh and tell him he could not plant on solid rock. Then Anancy would demand all the food the farmer was taking to market, because he claimed had been disrespected.

Sister Peel-Head Fowl picked up on his trick, so she told him she was going to the salon to get her hair done for the dance. Brer Anancy laughed at the bald woman. She immediately bawled out that he was disrespecting her and she demanded all the farmers' food back. She was the only one who was able to trick Brer Anancy and get back at him for all the jokes he had played on the people in the district.

Satisfied with the Anancy story, we went to bed. It was a long time before Momma came in. She reached over to turn down the fire of the little tin-can lamp that sat on a pile of suitcases. Finally, she lay down between us in the double bed. I relaxed and drifted into sweet sleep.

"What's that?"

I jerked out of slumber at Momma's voice. Eyes wide, I stared up into the dimly lit room.

Then I heard it—the sound of knives and forks hitting against plates repeatedly, as if people were in our front room having a feast. I began to shiver. I sidled closer to Momma, whose body was as rigid as a steel bar. She was wide-awake, too, listening to every clack of cutlery.

Then we began to hear voices, many different kind of voices, chattering away. And then we heard footsteps, as if people were walking around in the front room. One of those footsteps sounded like someone walking in spike heels. Click, click, click, they went. I could hear it in the outside hallway. Then the sound came closer into the middle hallway. They were coming closer and closer until they stopped right in front of the door to Momma's room. Behind this closed door Momma, Donna and I lay trembling.

I felt like my heart stop. I slid closer to Momma, pressing against her back. In bed, I lay at the back, closest to the window and I was terrified some evil spirit would reach in and grab me. My palms were damp with sweat as I clung to my grandmother. Donna was the one who lay facing the door but she didn't make a sound—she was the bravest little girl I knew.

"Don't come in here," Momma shouted. "I rebuke you in the name of Jesus. Get out of here and don't come back."

For a while there was silence—a silence so long I began to wonder if I had dreamt it all. Could it be that I was simply trapped in a nightmare? Had I imagined it? I prayed that this was so.

My prayer was not answered, because the silence was suddenly shattered with the sound of cutlery rattling in the living room. Forks, knives, spoons and plates began to clatter. The sounds coming through our bedroom door loud and clear.

I don't know how any of us survived that night. For the entire time that it was dark, right until the sun fought through and dispelled the darkness, the three of us lay like frozen mummies in the bed, unable to do anything but listen to the chattering, the spike heels pacing back and forth.

When the sunlight finally shone through our bedroom window, Momma and I rose up from our pillows. I looked across at Donna's sleeping body over at my grandmother. Neither one of us said a word.

When we finally opened the bedroom door and gingerly stepped into the living room, we could see no evidence that anyone had been feasting in our house. In fact, there was no sign that anyone had been there at all, except for the curtains.

This time it was even worse. Before they were simply pushed aside, but this time the red cloths hung crookedly, looking like drunken companions beside the serenely hanging sheer cream ones. The spirits really did not like Momma's red window coverings.

That evening, as the sun began to make its usual exit behind the curtain of the hills, Donna and I trudged into the house with our hearts quaking. Tonight there was no joking, no racing to get to the bed first, no begging Momma for ghost stories. Tonight we were afraid.

Momma locked the doors and windows tight, then ushered us into the bedroom where she made sure that the room door was closed. This time she did not turn the tin lamp down, but left it burning strong. Weak with apprehension, we crawled into bed.

Tired was I, but I was determined not to fall asleep that night. Whatever was out there, I was not going to let it sneak in on me. I lay in the stillness, listening to Donna's deep breathing, listening to my grandmother's silence, but I knew she was wide awake. I could sense she was just as scared as we were.

Eventually, sleep came to claim me. Slowly and surely, I slid deeper and deeper into the soft cotton candy of slumber.

Then it happened again. The chattering began in the front room, low at first, then louder and louder. The sound penetrated my dreams, bringing me back sharply to the present. Soon the dinner party was in full swing. In the midst of the chattering, the knives and forks began to clack.

Then the sound of the wretched spike heels. My back stiffened as I listened to them tapping against the creaky floor just like the night before, the strange presence in our home kept walking in the middle hallway, coming closer, closer to our bedroom door. I didn't open my eyes this time. I didn't want to see anything or hear anything. I just wanted this thing to go away.

Momma clutched Donna and me in the bed and started shouting: "Satan, I rebuke you in the name of the Father, Son and Holy Ghost."

But the noises did not stop. All night the voices kept chattering, the heels kept clicking and forks and knives kept banging against the plates. By the time daylight peeped in through the window, I had a throbbing headache.

This continued for many nights. In the mornings, I could see the stress on Momma's face.

Then one night, I saw a change in Momma's demeanor. Her face was grim and set. As she had done each night before, she locked all the outer doors and windows, then closed our bedroom door before we went to bed.

Within minutes the ghostly noises began. When the footsteps stopped just outside, Momma reached over to the nightstand and picked up the little lamp. "Come, we have to see what is going on."

My heart leaped to my throat and the terror choked me. Did I hear right? Was she really saying we should go and face the evil out there?

"This is my house; come on Blossom." It was the voice of determination. Momma may have been afraid, but this time she was not running away. I could see that she had reached her limit. Whatever was happening in our house, it would have to end.

Donna and I slid out of the bed. I went to stand behind my grandmother and Donna stood at her side. Momma grasped the doorknob and turned it. Slowly, she swung the door open.

"God the Father, God the Son, God the Holy Ghost," she chanted, as we faced the shadows ahead. Moving slowly, putting one foot in front of the other, she proceeded into the front room with Donna and me, clinging to her as she continued to chant, "God the Father, God the Son, God the Holy Ghost."

The living room, dark at first, was soon filled with light from the flickering fire in the can. It cast our shadows, tall and black, against the wall. Sheltered behind my grandmother's body, I peered into the room, seeing our furniture as we had left it with but ourselves in the room.

Then the light went out, as if some invisible person had blown it out, plunging us into total blackness. A scream ripped from my throat. I heard Donna's shriek echoing mine.

"Blossom, go bring me the matches."

Me? Leave Momma and go back into the pitch-black bedroom all by myself? I was shaking with fear. But Momma had spoken and she was waiting.

Feeling like I was going to my own execution, I backed away, leaving the safety of Momma's back to sidle into the dreadful blackness behind us. I was sweating the entire time I was in that room, feeling around on top of the pile of suitcases and desperately searching for the box of matches.

Finally, my hand hit upon the box. I rushed as quickly as I could in the dark, back to my grandmother's side. I gave the box of matches to Momma and she struck a match. Light flared instantly, sharp and bright, and Momma's face, scared and brave, came into view. Then poof ! The light disappeared, plunging us back into darkness. My heart jerked so hard inside my chest, I felt I would faint.

Momma struck another match. Again, someone—the spirit that was in the room—blew it out.

Four times Momma struck a match and four times our tormentor blew it out. Momma did not strike any more matches that night. We retreated as one back into the bedroom and shut the door. Immediately the ominous noises started again. We suffered through it for the entire night.

I guess Momma decided that the spirit was too strong for us to fight. Next evening, she packed us all up and we went to stay at uncle Beb's house for the night.

When Momma went to church, she told the pastor what was going on in her house. "Burn some white candles," he told her.

We went back to the house and did just as he said. We put a candle in a saucer with some water in the middle of the house and left it to burn. Next morning, we saw only an empty saucer. The candle had burned out with no wax left behind—no evidence that a candle had been in the saucer at all. And even with the white candles, the hell still went on every night.

More than one night, we tried to confront the spirit, but it was too strong. We just could not overcome it. Finally, the torment was more than we could tolerate. In the middle of the night, Momma made us get up and dress. "I am coming outside in the name of God the father, God the son and God the Holy Ghost," she said. It was 2 a.m. when we stepped out of the house and into night air that felt cold as death. A short distance away Momma looked back.

"Oh, my Lord," she cried out, "my house is burning down. Jesus Christ, everything is burning up in there."

Donna and I looked back and saw that our house engulfed in bright orange flames.

All we could do was turn and hurry on until we got to uncle Beb's house. "Beb," Momma called out, "Beb, the house is burning down."

It was as if uncle Beb had been expecting us. He quickly opened the door and ushered us in. He gave us sheets and told us to lie down, cover up and get some sleep. *No sense in going now* must have been his thought; because he too went back to bed. He probably thought it didn't make sense to go up there. After all, what could he do at that point?

Uncle got up at the crack of dawn the next morning to check on the damage. When he got back he asked, "Momma, what did you say happened last night?"

"My house burned down," she said.

"No," he said, shaking his head. "The house is still there. Nothing is wrong with it."

"What?" Momma looked at him as if he were mad.

We got our things and quickly followed uncle Beb back to the house. We were shocked to see it standing there, tranquil and whole, as if absolutely nothing had happened the night before. The spirits must have created an illusion, making us think the house had burned down.

As if all of this was not bad enough, we were also being attacked by a plague of rats. Every evening at about five-thirty, the yard would fill up with rats. There were so many of them, every patch of land around the house were covered by the rodents we had to seek refuge in the house and, even then, they were everywhere, scurrying along the window ledges and covering the floor. The only place we could escape them was on the bed.

For some reason and, much to our relief, they never tried to come onto the bed to attack us. Still, I can remember lying on the mattress, looking up at the ceiling and watching those rats running along the beams. I kept staring up at the ceiling, so scared that they would fall on me, begging when this nightmare would end.

Even with the advent of the rats, the spirits feasting and stomping around in our house at night never stopped. And so we existed, fending off rats and listening to ghostly parties at night.

With all that we were enduring, my grandmother decided that she was going to tell Uncle Enos what was going on. She wrote him a letter with all the haunting details.

"Enos, it is hard for me to be in my house," she wrote. "Every night I have to endure ghostly parties in the house. When I go to check what's making all the noise, by the time I open the door something blows out the light from the lamp. Each time I try to relight it, it is blown out again. There are footsteps coming to my bedroom door and, some nights, I have to go and sleep at your brother Beb's house. All this started when we received the box of clothes that you gave to me at your wife's funeral." Momma completed the letter and sent me to the post office to mail it off to Uncle Enos.

In the meantime, Momma consulted Minister Powell in regards to the ghostly activities. Momma was advised to "Get those clothes out of the house," he demanded. We got the box from the bedroom and took it to the outhouse. But that ended up not being such a good idea. When we wanted to go to the toilet, it was like there was a beast in there. Down in the hole we would hear all kinds of strange noises. We would all make sure to visit the outhouse in the daytime when things were quiet, but none of us would set foot in it at night when the sounds would start—sounds which were like a rolling calf snorting in the night.

We had to endure all this until one day we got a letter from America. It was uncle Enos replying to Momma. "Paste this paper on the front door," he wrote. In the envelope was the strangest piece of paper I had ever seen. The letters written on it looked like the number three turned face down, or like a series of the letter *m* clustered together—these strange symbols filled the entire page.

Momma did not question Uncle's instruction or the paper that he'd sent. She immediately got paste and stuck it on the front door. To everyone's surprise, the ghostly activities stopped as suddenly as they had started. That night, there was no more talking, there were no more footsteps, no sounds of dining and no rats. Finally, all was peaceful.

Pastor reached the conclusion that the spirit of my grandfather, Momma's husband, had seen this strange woman in the yard with us and so he brought down his compatriots to defend us. That strange woman was my aunt Megan. The spirit of Aunt Megan went back and got her cronies and so there seems to have been a battle of sorts among the spirits. Whatever happened, we were just glad to get rid of them all and get back to our lives as usual.

## V

For me, however, life was not destined to be the same because of one little problem—Donna. As time went by, the little girl became a thorn in the once serene relationship with Momma before her arrival. She was such a tattletale and it always caused tension with my grandmother. I just could not take it any longer.

During the Christmas holidays, Momma took us on a trip to Kingston to visit her daughter Emma. Christmas in the country was so different from Christmas in the city. In Marlborough at Christmas time, Momma would make a special trip to the market, and cook special meals for us. For the holiday, there was lots of meat on the table—beef, pork and chicken. Momma would also do some baking. We had a variety of food at Christmas time, which we were unable to eat it all. At our house, I did not get gifts for Christmas, but Momma would bring me something special from her shopping. I looked forward to getting candy and treats.

In our district for the holiday season, a merry-go-round was set up for the children. Parents would bring their little ones from all over the community to have fun and celebrate Christmas with playing and laughter. Because church was such an important part of Momma's life, we would also go there for Christmas celebrations.

On special occasions like this, there would be a concert, where members of the church recited poems accompanied by song. Momma loved going up to recite one of her favorite poems. I enjoyed the concerts, but was too shy to participate.

It was while at Aunt Emma's place in Kingston when I first saw the Jonkunnu dancers in the street. When you heard the drums beating, the flutes playing and people walking in droves along the street, you knew that it was Jonkunnu masqueraders coming. There was lots of shouting in the street as the band played. Children screamed and ran for their mothers, frightened by the masks of the horseman, as well as the bull and the devil. There was a man on stilts, so tall; he stood meters above everybody else. There was also a man dressed up as a police officer, another man dressed in drag and one dress as a wild Indian.

In the middle of it all was Pitchy-Patchy—a character decked out in a suit of colorful strips of cloth hanging all about. Pitchy-Patchy was covered from head to toe in red, green, yellow, orange, blue and multi-colored strips of cloth. Finally, the band brought up the rear with drums beating and horns tooting so that you could not even hear yourself think. Christmas in the city was very exciting.

During my stay in Kingston, I found my aunt to be loving and supportive of me. When it was time for us to return home, I grew somber—Aunt Emma saw my sadness.

"One of these days I'll come to the country and get Blossom to spend some time with me," she said to Momma.

I was delighted when I heard that. I could hardly wait for the day when she would come get me.

In the meanwhile, I did my best to stay out of Donna's way. I spent more and more time with my friend Princess. She had come from Hanover to live with her aunt, who had a grocery store in Marlborough. She was a little older than I was. I began leaving the house and going to spend time with her, as she helped out in the shop. She and I soon became good friends. I could always talk to her and she could always talk to me.

Princess and I developed a great friendship. I can remember her aunt calling us Sycki & Trim meaning we were always together if I am not in school. Until eventually she found a boyfriend by the name of Wilson, but we called him Brigo. He was tall—approximately six feet or so—dark and handsome. Princess had to keep her love interest a secret, because her aunt objected at her having a boyfriend. Therefore, I was the one who would take messages back and forth from Princess to Brigo, to keep the peace between Princess and her aunt. After a while, I found out that Princess was pregnant, carrying Brigo's baby. I was very happy to hear this, especially when Princess promised that I would be the baby's godmother. Her aunt was devastated by the news, but at this point, there's nothing she could about it. The way I saw it, Princess was mature enough to be a mother; she finished school and was working.

During Princess' pregnancy, we were always together—I was honored to be with her at such a special time and I could tell she appreciated by her support. Whenever we were together, she was always taking care of me by making sure I was fed and comfortable. Because of her generosity towards me, I developed a very strong friendship and love for her and her unborn child. Momma was quite happy that Princess was my friend. She was never worried because she always knew where I was. If I did not do my chores before leaving home, Momma could just go down the road and yell for me to come home and do them.

I remember one morning I was in my yard and I heard Mrs. Rob—Princess' aunt—calling me: "Blossom, Blossom . . . come! Princess is having the baby!" she exclaimed. I raced over the rocky hill to Mrs. Rob's home to see Princess and my new goddaughter. When I entered Princess' room, there she was—a cute and tiny little baby girl whom I got to hold. At this point, Princess reiterated that I was the godmother. I was, just thirteen years old and thrilled I was holding my godchild. I was a constant figure at Mrs. Rob's home after the baby arrived, helping Princess out in whatever way I could. At this point, I went out and bought my goddaughter some little dresses.

By this time, Brigo's Sister Brenda—now a proud auntie—begun to spend alot of time with Princess and her baby. I began to feel left out because Brenda was the aunt and I was just the godmother. We were all just so in love with baby Crystal and we could not get enough of her.

A few months later, Aunt Emma kept her word. She came to the country and took me back to Kingston to her house in Barbican. Aunt Emma was known in the community as a *Mother*—a healer of the sick and a religious woman. She would take my cousin and me to stand on street corners in the city and preach the gospel, shaking the tambourine and singing. She even had her own church in the community of Grants Pen. She was forever busy during these days, attending to the numerous church members and people of the community who would come to see her with their various problems. Some of them came to seek advice, while others came for healing.

I was happy to be with my aunt because she had taken me from the country and allowed me to experience life in the city. At Aunt Emma's, I used to cook, clean and wash—I was not afraid to work. I did everything she asked me to do, but I still needed more practice with cooking. Once when I prepared the mincemeat, burning it in the process, my aunt got angry and threw it out. I felt bad, because I was trying my best to impress Aunt Emma. However, I continued to work hard at it and, in the end, the experience in her kitchen served me well. Aunt Emma was the person who made me the cook I am today. While I was staying with Aunt Emma, I met one of my aunts who were visiting from England. Her name was Aunt Bernice—became close to her almost immediately. She was Momma's fourth child and, in my opinion, one of the prettiest. She had no children of her own, so she bestowed her love upon her nieces and nephews. She was such a beautiful woman, who had an accent that I could listen to all day. I had never heard anything like it and thought it was so refined.

Aunt Bernice was staying at her brother's house, but she made time to visit us. For some reason, she showed an interest in me that made me feel special. Aunt Bernice must have noticed I needed help, because I was no longer in the care of my grandmother. She knew my mother was not offering any assistance raising me and

Aunt Emma was inconsistent in my upkeep. "When I get back to England, I will send you some clothes," she told me. I could not believe it. I was very happy for her thoughtfulness because I desperately needed new clothes.

Aunt Bernice's visit to Jamaica passed much too quickly.

I had grown so attached to her that I knew I would miss her terribly. I made sure to be at the airport to see her off.

However, it was as if fate planned things otherwise. In the end, it seemed that I was not going to be able to fulfill my promise to my aunt. Aunt Emma left early in the morning to run some errands that day. The plan was that she would be back for us to get to the airport on time to say goodbye to Aunt Bernice.

But by 2 p.m., Aunt Emma did not return. I was not really worried initially, because I was thinking we had time to get to the airport—after all, it was only a half hour ride away. Two-thirty came and I remember telling myself to calm down. Three o' clock came, and then I started to worry, pacing the room, wondering what could have happened to her. By a quarter passed three, I was frantic. At this point, I was crying and no one was able to console me. I wanted so desperately to see Aunt Bernice before she left—and nothing anyone said was of any comfort unless I was taken to the airport. There was no way I would get to see Aunt Bernice now. The plane would lift off at 4 p.m.

By the time Aunt Emma drove into the yard, I became hysterical. She jumped out of the car and came to me, but I could not stop weeping. When she realized that nothing could stem the tide of tears, she bundled my cousins and I into the car and took off for the airport. Never had I seen my aunt drive so fast—within minutes she pulled up into the parking lot of the airport.

We dashed out of the car and into the terminal, then up the stairs to the waving gallery. Panting, I ran over to the railing and looked out onto the tarmac—a line of people was already heading towards the plane. But where was Aunt Bernice? My eyes skimmed the crowd—spotted my beloved Aunt Bernice and I waved my arms wildly.

"Aunt Bernice! Aunt Bernice!" I yelled. "I'm here!"

To my greatest joy, I saw her lift her hand and wave at us. My heart swelled with joy when I saw her turn her face up towards where we stood. Aunt Emma made my day and I was very thankful she got me there in time to see Aunt Bernice leave.

A few weeks after my aunt's departure, we received a letter from her, stating she had arrived safely and had a wonderful time in Jamaica. She also stayed true to her promise—I received a package filled with beautiful clothes from England.

One day in late January, Aunt Dearest—my mother—came to visit Aunt Emma. By this time, my mother had already given birth to three other children—Martha, Abraham and John—and was almost due to have the fifth child.

The reason for her visit was, not to invite me to her home to get to know my other siblings or as her daughter, but simply to get me to babysit the kids so she could go to the hospital to give birth.

"Can you allow Blossom to come over?" I overheard her asking Aunt Emma. "I need her to stay with the kids—it's almost time for me to check into the hospital."

I have never had a relationship with my mother to the point where I was comfortable enough to be around her alone. Asking me to stay in a strange place with three rambunctious children was too much to ask of me. Whenever Momma and I would visit they would walk on top of all the furniture, instead of the floor, and they never sat still. That was the reason our visits to my mother's house were often cut short.

"No," I told my aunt. "I don't want to go." She made no effort in pushing, because she understood I did not have much of a relationship with my mother therefore, I did not have to go.

After that, my mother made my life a living hell. For the two years I stayed with Aunt Emma, she constantly tried to pick fights with me. Even when Aunt Emma and I moved to the new house she built in Six Miles, mother would come there and try to hit me. She threw sticks at me and once she even threw a bucket at me.

While Aunt Emma was living in Barbican, she built a six-bedroom house in Six Miles with three bedrooms on either side of an enormous living and dining room. She even had her own maid quarters, both outfitted with their own kitchens, where she rent out one side to her daughter, husband and two children.

One particular day with no warranted provocation, my mother cornered me in the laundry room near the maid quarter—I don't remember what she was arguing about. In fact, I thought everything was fine between us, but it took nothing to trigger rage in my mother towards me. Back then anything her hand could touch, she would throw at me.

Mother never stopped causing problems for me. One day, she told my aunt I was gossiping about her to her youngest brother, Vincent. "You don't know what she is saying about you," she told my aunt, advising her to kick me out of her home. "She's telling people how she's seen you hugging up and kissing a man at the old house," she said, while scowling at me.

"What?" Aunt Emma turned to me with shock and disappointment stamped all over her face.

To my surprise, Aunt Emma no longer paid any attention to me. She stood there, staring at my mother. Her frown now turned to Aunt Dearest. Much to my relief, I realized then the spat between the two sisters had nothing to do with me. Seems like Aunt Emma was aware of what my mother was trying to do to me.

"Yes, yes," my mother continued, oblivious to Aunt Emma's mounting anger. "She says she's seen you with a man. And whatever happens in the house, she tells Vince

The thunderclouds set in Aunt Emma's face. Then she started to shout. "Yes? And you . . . you had an abortion." She turned to me. "She had an abortion, Blossom. There was another kid after you, but she aborted it. You were not the only child."

She fixed Aunt Dearest with a glare full of fire. "Blossom was not the only child," she declared. "You had another one after Blossom."

My mother froze and her eyes widened, as she stared at my aunt. Then she looked over at me. "Blossom, I never had an abortion. I never had an abortion."

I could say nothing. All I could do was stare back at her, my mind reeling in confusion thinking: Why *was she telling me this? Why was she defending herself to me? Wasn't she the one who had just been telling Aunt Emma to kick me out? What was really going on between her and auntie?*

In all the confusion, I could only guess what had happened. My cousins and I had peeped through a crack in the house and that is when we saw Aunt Emma and her gentleman friend fooling around. Seeing this really caught me off guard, because I thought that Aunt Emma was—or supposed to be—a spiritual leader in the community. Thus, quite naturally, I told my Uncle Vincent about it and he too was taken aback by the news. I guessed Uncle Vincent must have told my mother what I had confided in him, because she too was also staying at the old house in Barbican. That was why she was here that day at my aunt's new house in Six Miles, demanding she kick me out. This was her weapon—her way of getting back at me for reasons I do not know.

I was surprised Aunt Emma was angrier with my mother than with me. I expected her to ask me to leave, but instead she told my mother to pack her things and leave her home. The next morning, much to my relief, my mother gathered all her belongings and headed to the bus stop.

Nevertheless, life with Aunt Emma was far from perfect. There were things I endured which, even now, are difficult to accept while we were living in Barbican. While we were there, Aunt Emma allowed me to sleep in her bed every-so-often. I always wore a long nightgown to bed but it would not always cover me properly. As I slept, the silky fabric would sometimes ride up my legs leaving me partially exposed. One night as I lay sleeping in her bed, I felt the warmth of her body against my back—her breath tickling the hair on my neck. Then I felt her pressing her pubic area against my bottom. I knew it was that part of her because I could feel the wiry hairs against my skin. I could not move. I could not get up or do anything. I just lay there as if I were dead—no feelings, no emotions. I did not know what to do.

In the morning, I awoke feeling so ashamed and dirty. I did not want to speak to Aunt Emma. I got up and went underneath the house, which was set on stilts. There was lots of room for me to seek refuge under there. All morning I sat under the house, rocking myself back and forth deep in thought, reliving the nightmare of the night before. *Had I dreamt the whole incident? It could not have been real, could it? I could not reconcile such behaviour with my dear Aunt Emma in my mind.* Yes, I tried to convince myself, it must have been a dream, even though it seemed so real. But still, I was unable to leave my place of refuge underneath the house. All I could do was sit there and hug myself, rocking back and forth the whole time.

"Blossom, what are you doing under there?"

I did not look up at the sound of my aunt's voice. I could not face her. I was still too afraid and ashamed.

"Come and have your breakfast." Her voice was so calm, so normal. She did not seem the least bit disturbed or uncomfortable. I, on the other hand, was the one racked with guilt and shame.

She called out to me again and, this time, I slowly crept out of my hiding place. It had definitely been a dream, I decided. I would put it behind me, if I could, and not speak to anyone about it.

One day, sometime after this trauma, my mother came to visit Aunt Emma. They were sitting in the living room talking when I heard my mother telling Aunt Emma how she had gone to an interview at the Canadian Embassy. Apparently, she had had a first interview, where they had asked her how many children she had. She said she told them she had four children. This caused a problem, because a couple of weeks later, she received a telegram instructing her to come in for another interview. She must have thought they were contacting her to collect her visa, they again asked her how many children she had. Again, she said four, even though by this time she had given birth to her fifth child.

"They asked: Are you sure?" she said to my aunt. "I told them, yes."

That's when they said: "How could you have four kids when we checked at the Registrar General Department in Spanish Town and saw that you have another child by the name of Myrtle Adalsa Morrison? Where is that child?"

"Oh! She died," mother replied.

I heard the whole conversation from a distance. My mother knew I could hear her, but she did not care. I stared at her in horror and it did not seem to faze her in the slightest. Did she wish that I had never been born? I could not remember my mother ever showing me love and affection. Now, at the age of sixteen, it was obvious to me she did not care for me at all. I could not believe she was so quick to say that I was dead.

According to my mother, the immigration officer then turned to her and said, "If Myrtle Morrison is dead, then you will have to produce the death certificate."

That was when she broke down and started crying and finally admitted that I was not dead. She told them that I was living with her sister who was taking care of me. They advised her that she would not be granted the visa at that time. They said she could not leave the country until I was well protected. This was the conversation I heard between her and my aunt. Those words will stay burned in my memory forever.

The immigration officer asked my mother to bring a letter from my aunt stating she was my caretaker. That was the reason why she had come to see Aunt Emma—to request that letter. My aunt wrote the letter, stating I was living with her and that all my needs were being met. With that letter, my mother finally got her long-sought visa. A few weeks later, she left for Canada to be with her husband.

At Aunt Emma's new house in Six Miles, my cousins and I were still responsible for a good portion of the housework. We had to do the cleaning, dusting and cooking, even though there was a part-time helper. At times, the cooking was difficult, as Aunt Emma seemed to find fault with everything I made. I had come a long way from how I used to cook while living in Barbican. I was slowly improving with practice. Sometimes it was frustrating because, although I was doing my best, my aunt would often find reasons to complain.

Soon after we moved into this new community, I began to attend church. I was sixteen years old and I needed something more in my life than just the drudgery of housework. I did not go out to dances or the movies. I did not have access to any form of entertainment. My entire life seemed to revolve around the house. I remembered, when I was with my grandmother, she was always taking me to church on Sundays or to prayer meetings during the week. It was at Momma's church that I met Minister Powell, who became such a strong influence in my life. I learned a lot about wrong and right from that pastor. After Sunday school, I would sit and listen attentively as he preached. I would listen to all the stories he told from the Bible. I admired how passionately he spoke about God and about living a good Christian life. The way he used to speak, with such faith and conviction, in regards to the coming of the lord I thought God would have come already.

Minister Powell scared me straight. I remembered listening to him as a child, drinking in the stories about heaven and hell. I did not want to go to hell. I grew up thinking, *I will be good. I want to go to heaven.*

Minister Powell's teachings guided my life and my thinking. As a child, he molded my mind and taught me the value of life. He used to say: "Don't throw yourself around, don't commit fornication, thou shall not steal. Thou shall not covet thy neighbour or do onto others as you'd have them do onto you," among other words of wisdom he used to admonish his congregation—young and old.

With all that Christianity embedded in me from a child, I was always leaning towards the church. So when I saw a tent set up in the community for a Pentecostal Crusade meeting, I was drawn to it.

Night after night, I attended the weeklong crusade, eager to listen to the word of the Lord. This church was where I felt comfortable—a place where I could learn about God and about living a good life. It was what I had grown up with and it was what gave me the most satisfaction.

One night the preacher did an altar call. "If you feel you are ready," he said, "come forward and give your heart to the Lord." He raised his hand and beckoned to the congregation once more. "If you feel that the time is right," he shouted, "come forward and give your heart to the Lord."

As his voice rose over the murmurs and sighs of the congregation, people began to get out of their seats. One by one they walked up the grassy aisle between the tightly packed chairs and went to stand in front of the preacher. I watched as they went up and my heart swelled inside me. With all that I believed, I felt that—like these people—I was ready. I got out of my seat and walked slowly up the aisle to the pulpit.

"Is there anybody here who wants to be baptized?" the preacher asked.

I raised my hand, and so did the others standing beside me. On an appointed day, all of us who had accepted the Lord were baptized. A feeling of happiness came over me and I had the feeling that things would change for the better.

Even after the crusade ended and the tent had been taken down, I continued to worship with the Pentecostal congregation. Each Sunday and during the week, I would leave my aunt's house and walk to the church, which was not far from where we were living. I was now a member of a church family. In the end, it was not Aunt Emma's church that I joined, but another that gave me a sense of satisfaction and wholeness.

Despite my newfound life as a Christian, things were not perfect for me. The reality was that, since I came to live with Aunt Emma, she had made no motivation to send me to school to further my education. I did not know what the inside of a school in Kingston looked like. This used to bother me, as I knew I was missing out. I used to admire the children in their uniforms as they passed by on their way to school—I always wished I could be one of them.

One day I decided that, even if I could not be a schoolgirl, I could start dressing like one—and that is what I did. Wherever I went, people would call out to me: "Hi, school girl." It pleased me.

Still, as I thought about my future, I was hopeful. I began to toy with the idea of finding myself a job. I needed so many things. I had the same basic needs of any other young girl, but Aunt Emma did not give me an allowance. Sometimes I would get depressed, not knowing where to go for help. Early one morning I got up and decided to go job hunting. At my age, I was thinking if I dressed professionally, the chances of me getting hired would be greater. So I wore one of the outfits Aunt Bernice sent me from England. I headed out to the youth employment centre on Orange Street in downtown Kingston to see if someone could help me find a job. I was surprised to find that there was already a long line of young people waiting outside. It did not deter me, so I took my place at the end of the line.

I stood there, patiently waiting my turn, when a gentleman approached me. I had seen him outside the employment centre for some time and assumed that, like me, he was waiting to get a job. He was a light-skinned young man, clean cut and well dressed. He seemed like a decent person.

"You're looking for a job?" he asked.

I told him I was.

"Do you know those new buildings in the Half Way Tree area? I know people who work over there. I can get you a job." He tipped his chin towards me. "Come with me," he said. "I will take you there."

I was elated to hear this good news, because I was starting to become weary of my chances of employment seeing the long line of people who seemed more qualified than I. As I followed the gentleman, I began daydreaming about getting my first paycheck, being independent and, for the first time, being able to buy all that I needed.

I was walking along the road with him when I noticed the clothing in his hand. They were in clear plastic, so it seemed he had just picked them up from the dry cleaner.

"If you don't mind, I want to make a quick stop by my house to drop off my clothes," he said. "After that we can head straight to Half Way Tree."

I did not object. We continued walking until we got to a brick, two-story building with a verandah and lots of windows. A fence encircled the building. We stopped at the front gate.

"Just stay out here and wait for me," he said. "I won't take long."

I stood at the gate, waiting patiently for his return. I was outside for about ten to fifteen minutes before he came back outside.

"You can come and sit on the verandah. This will take me a few minutes, so come and have a seat."

I did as he asked, leaving the side of the road to go up the driveway and onto the verandah. A few more minutes passed and, again, he popped out to talk to me. "Come into the house. I want to show you something."

Warning bells suddenly went off in my head. "No, its okay," I replied. "I'll wait here."

A scowl darkened his face when he heard my refusal. "Come in," he repeated, more forcefully this time.

I shook my head, intending to leave as quickly as I could. Before I could make a move, he grabbed me around the waist and began to drag me towards the door.

"Let me go!" I yelled, fighting to get away from his hold. By this time, I knew that this man meant me no good. If he got me through the door, I would probably end up being raped or even killed.

I was screaming, punching and kicking, struggling to get out of the man's grasp. As I called out for help, a host of people were suddenly in the corridor staring at us, watching all that was happening. I screamed some more but nobody came to my rescue.

"She's my girlfriend," the man yelled out, even as he dragged me towards the door. In a flash, everybody had disappeared.

The man pulled me towards the door, trying to get me inside. I saw a round table with a glass of water on it, a stool and a well-made bed. He was already inside, but I was still outside bracing myself against the doorjamb, fighting hard to break away from his hold. He became so enraged that he reached over, picked up the stool and attacked me with it, hitting my arms as I tried to deflect the blows aimed at my head. It was only then did I loosen my grip on the door.

The man dragged me into the room, but I tore out of his grasp and ran. I was fleeing blindly, through the side door, from room to room, not knowing where I was going, but trying desperately to find an escape. The man ran after me, grabbing my blouse, but I escaped as the clothes ripped in his hand.

I barreled towards another room and he grabbed at me again, but all he got was another piece of my clothing. My breath coming in gasps, I kept fleeing in terror. I was able to put some distance between me and my attacker. I dashed into a room and there was an old woman sitting with a child in her arms. She must have known that something was wrong because of my disheveled state.

Quickly, she beckoned with her head, pointing me in the right direction. I bolted past her, and burst through a door and headed down a flight of stairs into the backyard of the building. I took off and raced around the side of the building until I saw the road in front of me. I ran and ran, and did not stop running until I ended up all the way down the street, at a bus stop some distance away.

Panting, I looked back. Was he following me? My heart pounded with fright, but there was no one in sight. My heart was still racing and I was breathing hard as I waited anxiously, praying for the bus to come. The entire time I was waiting, I kept looking up the road towards the building, petrified I would see him running towards me.

Finally, the bus pulled up in front of the stop and I jumped on—relief washed through my body, making me weak. It was then that I realized that I had no handbag, no money, not even bus fare. I began to explain to the driver what had happened to me. When I looked at myself in his rearview mirror I was shocked at how tattered I looked. My clothing was ripped and I had welts and scrapes all over my body. I guess that was all the evidence the driver needed, because he did not question my story. He let me sit in the bus and we were on our way.

When I got home to Aunt Emma's house, I was still trembling. I wanted to tell her. The words were fighting to burst out of me, but I could not do it. My aunt had no idea I had gone job hunting. If I told her what had happened, I did not know what her reaction would be.

In the end, I swallowed the story, bottling it up inside me. It was not until a few days later that I told a friend of mine what had happened. When I told her where the building was located, she told me the place was not a house, but a motel. Young and naïve, I had followed the man to a place where he could have taken advantage of me. As I relived the ordeal in my mind, I felt surprised that I had not even thought of reporting the incident to the police.

I learned my lesson well. My near rape experience traumatized me to the point where I could not travel, night or day, without feeling like I was being stalked. Never again would I put my trust in a stranger.

## VI

Although Aunt Emma had written the letter to the Canadian Embassy, assuring them she was taking care of me, in less than a year, she began making plans to immigrate to the USA. Eventually, I knew I had to move again, so I began to ask among my relatives for a place to stay. During the course of trying to find a place, my aunt got married, packed up and left Jamaica to join her husband in the USA. At the age of seventeen, I had nowhere to stay.

To my great relief, Aunt Emma's daughter, Megan, agreed for me to stay with her and her family. I stayed there for just a short while. During that time, I helped with the housework and babysitting her children. Each night, Megan had me set her hair in rollers, which became a regular nightly routine that I did not enjoy. But, things became a bit uncomfortable for me when Megan and her husband began to have problems.

Eventually, I went to live with Aunt Eunice in Spanish Town. Aunt Eunice was the daughter of Momma's sister, and of Momma's late husband Josiah. Aunt Eunice's mother was living with her, and I ended up staying in her room. There were two beds in the room, one for her and another that I shared with Aunt Eunice's little boy.

At this house, little did I know that a new nightmare was about to begin.

One night I awoke to the disturbing feeling of a hand caressing my breast. I was stunned to see a man standing over me—it was Aunt Eunice's husband. My grandaunt realized what was happening and tried to defend me.

"Why don't you leave the child alone?" she shouted. Even though the man must have thought she was just a senile old woman, she was very coherent of what he was doing. "What are you doing in here? Get out and leave the child alone!"

This happened night after night, but I was too afraid to say anything to Aunt Eunice. Finally, just the thought of him entering my room every night, was too unbearable and one day I just got up and left. This time I went to stay with my Uncle Kevin, who was Aunt Eunice's brother, and his family. I had visited his home many times before, so he was no stranger to me. When I got to his house, I was surprised to see my little sister, Suzette. My mother must have left her there when she departed for Canada.

Not long after I arrived, I was alone in the house with Uncle Kevin—his children were out in the yard playing. To my horror, right there in one of the rooms, he grabbed me and pushed his tongue into my mouth. I had never experienced anything like that before and coming from my own Uncle! I was repulsed. *How could a blood relative do such a thing to me?* More than once, he grabbed me and tried to kiss my lips. I decided I could not stay there. I packed my few belongings and moved on. This time, I went to Aunt Icema's place and took Suzette with me. I was afraid to leave her unprotected at Uncle Kevin's. I could not let her face the same abuse that I had suffered. At least at Aunt Icema's we should be safe.

At the time, Aunt Icema was living in a rented room, so there was not much space, but Suzette and I tried to fit in. The two of us slept with her on her double bed for the first few nights of our stay. At this point, I was very unsettled by what I had gone through while staying at Aunt Eunice's home. I ended up confiding in Aunt Icema about what had happen to me, which led me to the assumption that Aunt Icema must have told Aunt Eunice what I had said, because she later accused me of lying. We never spoke again since then.

One day, Aunt Icema's male friend came to visit her, whom she introduced him as her boyfriend, Mr. Clark. I remember Mr. Clark as Aunt Emma's friend who always came by the house. He was also a member of her church and played the guitar there as well. Mr. Clark was always wearing gabardine pants, which were not considered fashionable at the time.

Aunt Icema now made new sleeping arrangements to include Mr. Clark, because he was sleeping over. All four of us were to sleep on the one double bed. I ended up sleeping in the middle, with my head towards the foot of the bed, in the direction opposite to Aunt Icema and Mr. Clarke.

That same night I woke up to feel something pressing inside me. It was someone's finger. My body went rigid—I could not move. Shocked and confused, I could only stiffen my body to the invasion; I could not shift. I could not scream—all I could think was *it must be Mr. Clarke who was doing this*. I wanted to scream. I wanted to make a sound to alert my aunt that this was happening. But, I painfully chose not to alert her; because Aunt Eunice had called me a liar regarding a similar incident. Letting my Aunt know at this point what was happening would most definitely result in her kicking me out of her home with my little three-year-old sister.

The thought of needing a mother and having nowhere to go, except for going back to the country bothered me a lot. I felt I had more opportunities in the city in the hopes of making something of myself one day. So I laid there, scared, trying my best to make him stop by tensing my body and praying that he would leave me alone, without making any movement that would awake my aunt.

Following the event from the night before, I could not look Aunt Icema in the face. I felt so ashamed for what this man had done to me. With just his finger, he had stolen my innocence.

For the next few nights, I was on edge, but Mr. Clarke did not stay over again. Still, I concluded that I could not stay there anymore, not with the threat of having him return to do the same thing again—or worse.

"I'm going back to the country," I told my aunt.

Soon after, I began packing again, moving on like a rolling stone. The thought hit me that I would not be returning home to Momma as the young innocent girl she knew before I left; rather as a seventeen year old, young woman who was robbed of her innocence by people I trusted.

Back in the country, I was happy to be with my grandmother again and I was glad to meet my cousins Monica, Jenny, Janelle and Donna, who were now living at the house with Momma. A little later their sister Ruth came with her daughter, Carlene, who was the same age as Suzette. We had a house full of girls and this made me feel safer.

I was among a group of girls I could be myself around and enjoy life again. Best of all, I was far away from men who could not take advantage of me.

## VII

Even though we were staying with Momma, I took on the responsibility of caring for Suzette. There were times when she was often mistaken as my child, because wherever I went, I would bring her with me.

While I was in the country, I met a past schoolmate—Fitzroy. I used to see him sometimes when I would make quick trips back to the country with groceries Aunt Emma sent for Momma. Tall, light-skinned and about a hundred and eighty-five pounds—he was very handsome. He wore his hair in a big, black, curly afro and was always dressed in style. He had a lot of girls chasing after him because he was quite the looker.

Fitzroy was interested in my cousin Monica; but she was already seeing someone else. On one of his visits to see my cousin, he and I end up talking and, over time, we developed a friendship. I was not allowed to go on dates, so our relationship flourished every evening when he stopped to bring me ice-cream and other treats.

On occasion, Fitzroy would bring me peanuts which I was told enhances ones "sexual nature" and at the same time I was sucking on limes, because as a child I remember hearing that it decreases ones sexual desires. During the time when I had to run errands for

Momma, I would take Suzette along and Fitzroy would accompany me. At times, people mistook Fitzroy and me as Suzette's parents. Suzette was a very beautiful and shy child. She would only allow Fitzroy and me to hold her. The way Fitzroy interacted with my baby sister made me believe he was a loving and caring person; which made him even more attractive to me. As the relationship continued to develop, so did my love for him. I could neither eat nor sleep. I cried and laughed for no good reason—I always wanted to know where he was. It was as if I was going crazy for the young man, and through those emotions, I still did not know what a kiss was like. He wanted to kiss me and be physical, but I kept resisting.

Three months later, my mother wrote me a letter, telling me her husband wanted Suzette to be with her other siblings. They were with his mother in Glengoffe—a small town in the parish of Saint Catherine. I was sad to let Suzette go, but I had to respect my mother's wishes.

At night, young men lined the road, some of them sitting along the fence that barred the cows from roaming the streets. All these young men would come to see the girls in Momma's house, particularly Monica, Ruth and I, as we were the oldest ones.

Desmond, Sturdy and Fitzroy were our main visitors. Some of the other guys from the surrounding communities were pushy and they did not like how these three young men were making friends with us before they did, and because of this they started to make trouble for us by throwing condoms into our yard.

Momma's morning routine was to pray for her children, her grandchildren, her Pastor and congregation, the government and the world, asking God to grant them knowledge, wisdom and understanding. Then she would go to inspect the gate and check around. Once it was all clear, and to her liking, only then was she able to start her day. On one particular morning, after completing her routine check, Momma discovered condoms littering the front yard—there was no convincing her that we had not used those condoms with the boys. She became furious. Then when Uncle Beb came by the house, Momma told him what she found. He threatened to break the door down and come in and beat us.

"You are whores!" Momma shouted, unconvinced we had nothing to do with it. After what happened to me in Kingston, the last thing I ever wanted to be called was a whore, especially from my grandmother. I was not afraid of Momma finding condoms in the yard because I was not sexually active, but it distresses me so much to hear Momma make such a general statement calling us whores and surprised she would think so terribly of my cousins and I. Nothing we said could make her believe otherwise.

Momma started to write letters to her daughters overseas, informing them what she thought we were doing in her home. On hearing all of this, Aunt Bernice began to give me the cold shoulder—and then she turned her back on me. She was the last person on earth I wanted to think ill of me.

This was not my only problem. I noticed Fitzroy had a wondering eye. When we were together, he had eyes for no one else. When he was with me, he was totally with me; I was the only woman who seemed to exist for him then. But when he was out of my sight, it was another matter. It was just my bad luck to fall in love with a ladies' man. How could I have settled for a man who was not right for me at the age of eighteen? I was so naïve.

Because Momma has embedded it in my head about boys, I would not allow Fitzroy to touch me. Then one night, he stole a kiss. After he left, I went inside and ate a big meal then headed for bed. In the midst of changing into my sleepwear, what I saw gave me a shock—my stomach looked so big. I was convinced Fitzroy's kiss got me pregnant. I did not sleep at all that night. Luckily, by the next day, my huge meal had been digested and my stomach was back to normal. I breathed a sigh of relief.

One evening my grandmother sent me to the post office in Balaclava—I had to walk all the way. By the time I started home the shadows of night lurked in every corner. Nightfall in the country was so different from Kingston. At least in the city, streetlights soften the darkness and I could usher myself from one light to another. Here, darkness descended quickly, the night came soft, then thick and heavy. There were no streetlights to guide you along the way this time—I was on the road, all alone and afraid.

I hurried along the stony road, anxious to get back to the safety of Momma's yard. At every sound, I jumped; with every shadow that I saw in the bushes, my heart leaped into my throat. My walking turned to running. It was hard to keep up the pace. I slowed down when exhaustion hit, but I broke into a sprint again when I saw some bushes rustling beside me.

Soon, it was pitch black. My heart pounded in my chest and I felt beads of cold sweat trickle down my back. I kept on walking as fast as I could. I was about a mile and a half away from Balaclava when I realized I was at "V Curve," which was a deep curved road.

*What was I going to do? Should I dare go around the curve where the cars would drive, or should I take the shortcut and climb over the stones?* I decided to take the shortcut. There was no way I was going around that corner, not after hearing that area was haunted.

I climbed the stones as quickly as I could, looking straight ahead, avoiding the bushes and the trees. This was such a beautiful path during the day because of the shade the trees provided. People frequently stopped here to take in the view. At night, it was a scary place. There was a rumour that people who died would come back to haunt this spot. I could feel the goose bumps forming all over my body.

As soon as I got off the path and on to the main road, I set off again. I was about a mile away from home, when I heard footsteps behind me. I whirled around, but there was no one there. I took off running again, but I still heard the footsteps—and this time they were not walking, they were running behind me. I mustered the courage to look back over my shoulder as I ran but still I could see no one in the darkness behind me.

My breath coming in gasps, I ran faster and faster and yet the footsteps kept pounding behind me. Almost crazy with fear, I ran and ran, past all the places where people said ghosts lingered. My heart swelled with fright and I was exhausted, but I could not stop.

I ran and ran, and still the footsteps followed me on that dark, lonely road.

*Jesus, have mercy*, I thought, *can't somebody come and save me?*

Like an answer to my prayer I saw someone at the top of the road—someone coming towards me. I sprinted up to the figure in the distance—wanting only to be saved I ran right up to him, panting with fright and relief. It was Fitzroy.

The relief flooded through me and I began to laugh and sob at the same time, even with little air left in my lungs.

"What's wrong?" he asked, concern reflected on his face.

"Someone was running after me," I gasped, "trying to catch me."

He peered into the darkness behind me. "But there's nobody there."

"Yes," I said, still breathless, nodding my head. "Someone was following me."

Fitzroy took my hand—it was only then that the tightness in my chest loosened, the tension of fright, began to relax its hold and I could finally breathe again. Fitzroy kept holding my hand as we walked up the road together, down the hill and round the bend, right to Momma's house. I was so grateful to him. I later found out he had gone to my grandmother's house to see me but was told I had gone to Balaclava. When I ran into him, he had been on his way to meet me—it was the best thing he could have done for me that evening.

It was not all smooth sailing in my relationship with Fitzroy. A major problem was I had an uncle in the country that was very controlling. He did not like the idea of me dating. He was so protective that he did not even allow me to talk to boys. Fitzroy and I had to hide our relationship for a long time. Uncle Beb always had a sneaking suspicion we were dating and he often gave me a hard time about it. He would beat me whenever he saw us together.

At eighteen, I decided that I was not going to take it anymore. Moreover, Fitzroy was not his child. For my uncle to be threatening to beat him too; was unacceptable. We finally decided we were not going to hide our love any more.

One evening, we were both standing in front of Momma's gate. I was on the side where our house was and Fitzroy was by side of the road. We saw my uncle coming. He was on his way to church.

"I'm not moving," Fitzroy said as he watched the older man approaching.

"Me neither," I agreed, although my heart thumped with apprehension.

When Uncle Beb saw us, he barged up to Fitzroy, as if to hit him. Fitzroy stood to his full height, his hand shoved deep into his pocket. Uncle drew back and stared at Fitzroy with his hand still hidden in the pocket. He did not come any closer. Instead, he shouted at us, but then he went on his way. He must have thought Fitzroy had a knife or some kind of weapon in his pocket. That was the only reason I can think of as to why Uncle Beb left so abruptly. But I knew uncle was not going to let me off so easily.

"When I come back, I'm going to break the door down," he shouted. "I'm going to get you tonight."

Fitzroy said he had had enough. "Go pack your things," he told me.

For the first time in my life someone was standing up for me—apart from Momma—and I felt a sense of protection. He waited for me to get my clothes, and then he took me straight to his parent's house. He told his parents that my uncle wanted to beat me because I was dating him, and he did not want any part of it. He wanted me out of that house and somewhere safe, he told them.

That night I felt loved by his family. It was one of the first nights in my life that I felt special. Fitzroy's mother, Miss Clem, allowed him to sleep beside his Dad, while I slept in the bed with her and the rest of the children. There were so many children and all of them wanted to be close to me that night.

I woke up the next morning and Fitzroy's mother was making breakfast. When it was ready, I was the first to be served. Miss Clem had fourteen children—with maybe six or seven living at home—and yet she served me before anyone else. She treated me with so much love.

During the months that I stayed there, Miss Clem was forced to sit at the back during mass. Her church did not approve of my living with them without being married to her son. The people at church assumed that Miss Clem was allowing us to live in sin in her house. But little did they know, the entire time I spent in their house, Fitzroy and I did not even kiss.

Uncle Beb would have nothing to do with Miss Clem and her family. However, Miss Clem told me one day my grandmother thanked her for having me in her home. Momma knew I was safer at Miss Clem's. She knew very well what I could have suffered at my uncle's hands. Many times, when my uncle used to beat me, Momma was the one who would take me, lay me on the bed, and bathe the welts on my back with warm salt water. My grandmother understood that I was better off where I was.

My time with Miss Clem eventually ended. I had to go back to the city to prepare my papers. But before doing so, I went to say goodbye to Momma, as I would be going to Montreal with my brothers and sisters to join our mother and her husband. My mother had filed for her children to go to Canada to live with her.

It was very hard for me to leave Fitzroy, as we had grown very close. Now, realizing that I would not be seeing him again for a long time, I finally let my resistance down. We shared a kiss and, for the first time, we made love.

In tears, I left for Kingston. There, I stayed with Aunt Icema. Shortly after that, I left for Montreal. However, I could never forget Miss Clem and her family, or the kindness they had shown me for so many months. I left Jamaica with happy memories of being showered with love from a mother who was not of my blood.

# The Montreal Years

# VIII

On October 2, 1976, at the age of nineteen, I arrived in Montreal, Canada. My four siblings and I had taken the plane journey to this country to start a new life with our mother. As soon as we came out of the customs hall, Mother and her husband rushed over to the four younger ones and hugged them hard, laughing and giving them lots of kisses. I stood aside, watching. When they were finished, we got the bags and headed towards the exit.

I tried my best not to show my feelings, but inside I was filled with hurt. For me there was no hug, no smile, not even a hello. It was as if I was totally invisible to my mother. Swallowing my pain, I remained silent as I followed the reunited family to the car.

We arrived at my mother's apartment. My mother and her husband obviously were still filled with the excitement of having their children around her. They kept hugging them and asking questions about what they had been doing back in Jamaica. In the meantime, I was totally ignored.

A few weeks later, my mother relocated to another apartment across the street, which was bigger to accommodate her much larger family. As usual, we were relaxing with friends on the weekend, which became a regular event at our home. To my surprise, my stepfather must have noticed the cold shoulder I was getting from my mother. Out of the blue he called me over, "come here Blossom!" he then turned to mother and said, "Imo, give your daughter a hug; give your daughter a hug." In return my stepfather got a disapproving stare from his wife.

Nevertheless, it was only then that she turned and looked at me. It was almost as if she were seeing me for the first time. I could see that she did not like the idea of hugging me.

"Blossom, hug your mother."

At my stepfather's insistence, I approached her. I raised my arms and put them around my mother. At that instance my stepfather thought it was a Polaroid moment and snapped a picture. To my surprise, her arms hung limply at her side. She was making no attempt to return my hug. I stepped back, smarting at her rejection. I decided I would never try that again.

Soon after our arrival, Mother went shopping. It was cold, and we had little clothing that was appropriate for the weather. The children waited anxiously for her return. Within a few hours, we heard a horn tooting out front—it was Mother and she had returned in a taxi.

"Blossom," Mother called out, "come down and help me bring in the bags."

I hurried outside and approached the car when Mother opened the door my eyes widened, there were bags and bags filling the backseat. It looked like she had bought a whole store all by herself. I quickly grabbed as many of the bags as I could and took them inside then went out for more, it took me a few trips in order to empty the car.

Some of the bags were taken into the kitchen, while the other bags with clothes and toys were placed in the living room where the children were watching television. Then Mother went to sit on the sofa. She began to sort through the bags as she sorted; she called each of the children and gave them what was theirs.

"Here, Martha this is for you."

Martha eagerly went over to take the items a big smile spread across her face. Mother had not only bought her clothes, but some toys as well. "Thank you, Mommy," Martha said.

Mother then called Abraham. "Come, this is for you." She handed him his gifts, and he too thanked her happily.

Next, were Suzette and John—both of them were very excited. "Thank you, Mommy," they said, grinning from ear to ear.

All this time I was in the living room with them, I patiently listened for my name. As each of the bags disappeared, I sat expectantly, thinking that the next one would probably be mine. When the last item was handed out, I sat staring at the empty sofa where the bags had been—I felt a huge lump rise in my throat. I could not speak. I got up from the chair and slowly walked to the bedroom I shared with my sisters. I went in, closed the door behind me, and lay on the bed where a sob ripped from my throat. I put my fist to my mouth to stifle the sound.

Suddenly, I heard a horrible slam, and the door flew open. I jumped up off the bed. I stared at my mother as she stood glowering in the doorway. She had kicked the door open.

"You are not paying any rent in here," she shouted. "You have no right to close this door."

With that, she stormed away, leaving me staring at her stiff, unyielding back.

That night when my stepfather got home, he saw me in the bed with my sad face from the living room and realized that something was wrong. He called me and asked: "What's the matter, Blossom?" I shook my head; unable to muster a smile, but I said nothing.

"Mummy didn't buy Sister anything," one of the children piped up.

My stepfather turned to me. "Come here, Blossom," he said.

Slowly I approached him, tears stinging my eyes with the hurt still fresh in my mind.

He put his hand in his pocket and pulled out his wallet. He took out a twenty-dollar bill. "Here, Blossom. Go buy yourself something—whatever you want."

I stared up at him, shocked at his generosity. I could not believe he was giving me so much money. "Thank you," I said, biting my lip to hold back the tears of gratitude. However, I must interject: although my stepfather had his faults, he was not impartial when it came to treating the children fairly, including me. That week I went shopping and, by the time I was finished, I had a new dress for church, a pair of shoes, a handbag and change left over for my offering at church.

Now that I was living in Canada with my mother, I felt as though all the unresolved issues between us in Jamaica were still present. Therefore, there was nothing I would not do for her to keep the peace, I thought. However, despite all my efforts to make things work, Mother and I still could not get along—she was constantly fighting with me. Within a few months of my being in her home, she became openly hostile towards me. She would always stare at me, a cross look on her face, even though I had done nothing to annoy her. I was very uncomfortable in her home. I just did not understand why she was behaving this way towards me.

I thought I had left the nightmare of being harassed behind me in Jamaica, but it was not so—within a few months of me being in Canada, my stepfather started touching me inappropriately. At first, it started out as a few bumps here and there and then he started grabbing at my breast outright when no one was around. The unwanted advances he forced upon me revived the memories of all the abuse inflicted upon me by family members and family friends. Here I was seeking paternal care and attention, but instead I was constantly being terrorized by unwanted advances from my stepfather.

On the other hand, I could see how excited her husband was to have us. He would invite his friends over to show off his kids and, to my surprise, he would include me. However, there were some things that really bothered me. Once, while we were visiting some family friends, we noticed there was not enough seating for everyone. My stepfather invited me to sit on his lap, I reluctantly did so—I did not want to cause I scene. But my forebodings were correct, shortly after my stepfather started thrusting his pelvis, which made me very uncomfortable. I got up as soon as I found an excuse to do so.

My mother's neglect continued, as my babysitting and housekeeping duties superseded the importance of my going to school. I ended up staying at home and playing the role of nursemaid to my four brothers and sisters. I would get them up in the mornings, prepare their breakfast, get them ready for school and then have a hot lunch ready for them when they got home.

Taking care of the home and the children fell heavily on my shoulders. During the days, while my mother and her husband were out at work and the children were at school, I would clean the house, do everyone's laundry by hand and hang them on the line outside to dry. Neighbors would comment on my workload and praise me for my commitment. "Did you do all of this alone?" they sometimes asked—They often told me I had done a good job.

My mother's reaction was in stark contrast to everyone else's praise. She would come home from work and, on seeing the washed clothes; she would go straight to the clothesline and start taking them off one piece at a time. She would throw all the clothes on the ground then gather them up and take them down to the laundry room, where she would wash them all over again. She never said a word to me and never gave me a reason for her behaviour.

I felt so hurt that I would go to my room and put my hand on my head. All I could do was sit there and wonder: *Why me? How did she come to hate me so much?*

It also fell on me to take care of any issues the children had at school. Eventually, the principal told me I needed to stop being their parent and that I needed to be in school myself. I should at least attend night school, he told me. Those words of encouragement meant a lot to me. I knew I could not get myself through school just then, but it was a thought I now began to cherish in my heart.

As if things were not bad enough, my stepfather—who was a custodian at a nearby bank—started asking me to accompany him to work some evenings. He made it seem as if he needed help. I could guess what he was up to, so on the few occasions that I went; I found an excuse to take the children with me. At least with them around, he would not try anything, I thought.

My plan worked for a while, then my mother stepped in. to my surprise, she forbade me to take the children anymore. I could not believe it. If she had, any fear that I had interest in her husband; wouldn't she want the children there to prevent anything from happening? Or, at the very least, they could bring reports back to her if anything did happen.

"No, they're not going," Mother said in response to my query. "You go."

Her decision left me in a dilemma—even when the children were there, he would still try to touch me inappropriately. How was I going to avoid the advances of this man all alone with him in an empty building? That first evening when we went without the children, I had a hard time keeping him away from me. He kept trying to kiss me and I ended up running round inside the bank, trying to stay out of his clutches.

The fights with Mother got more frequent and more heated—as usual, the main cause was her husband. She constantly accused me of trying to steal him from her, no matter how I tried to avoid him.

Why, then, had she allowed us to go alone together to clean the bank those evenings? I could not understand it.

Despite my efforts, Mother had no kind words for me. To her, I must have seemed like a robot. I had been transplanted from Jamaica to this house in Montreal simply to serve the family. There was no love coming my way. Mother was not even interested enough to think about my basic needs. I was a young woman living in her home, penniless, but never once did she offer me money for my personal needs.

If it were not for her husband, I would have been in a sorry state. At least he thought of the fact that I would need change to cover my personal needs. For this kindness, I was grateful.

Arguments with Mother were never about cleaning the house or taking care of the children. She knew she could leave—there was no one else to maintain the house and keep the children clean and fed. In fact, I used to be able to control the little ones better than she herself could—they never listened to her. She would say: "Blossom, talk to them for me," when she knew she could not discipline them. They defied her and call her ugly Mommy. It did not take much from me telling them to behave themselves—I just had to look and everyone would be on their best behavior.

Although I tried my best to avoid my stepfather, things eventually got worse. On occasions, when mother was out or working, he would send the children to the park to play. On one particular day, he pinned me down in the couch trying to fondle me. The man was twice the weight I was, but it did not deter me from struggling to get out of his grip. I angrily pulled away, "I don't like what you're doing daddy," I told him. "Stop it daddy." Instead of being ashamed, he continued to make advances. I could not believe that my stepfather was acting in this manner. Here I was calling him daddy; eager to be part of the family, wanting a father, and this was how he was conducting himself. I often thought of telling my mother about it, but I guessed she would just use the information to start a fight. She would surely blame me for coming into her house and causing problems. I would later come to the realization that telling her would only create a bigger nightmare for me.

My mother continued to quarrel with me about her husband—she blamed me for his behaviour. She would curse me so much about him that, one day, I gave her a sharp retort. "Who wants your husband?" I shouted "Why would I want him, with his old drunken self? I have my boyfriend in Jamaica. I don't want your husband."

However, no matter how much I told her I had no interest in him, she kept on accusing me and picking fights.

Another thing Mother would do was talk badly about me to her friends who came over. She did not care whether or not I heard. Each time she would behave this way, all I could do was walk away and go to the bedroom. But even here, I had no refuge. I was not allowed to close the door so I stayed in the room knowing that, from where they sat in the TV room, all her friends could see me. I was stripped of all privacy and there was nothing I could do about it.

One night in particular, we had a big fight and she called the police. When they got to the house, my mother was still cursing me.

One of the police officers took me outside. "Who is that lady?" he asked.

"My mother," I replied.

With a surprising look on his face he asked, "Your mother?" He looked like he did not believe me. "Go—bring your passport and birth certificate. The passport is to prove you are a landed immigrant and the birth certificate to prove that she's really your mother."

I went and got them. While he reviewed my documents, the other police officer went to calm my mother down. After verifying that what I had said was true, the first police officer said: "You know you can't stay here."

"But where am I going to go?"

"You have to find somewhere. That lady is going to hurt you. You cannot stay here."

Not having anywhere to go and anyone to turn to, I had to go back upstairs to the room I shared with my two younger sisters. Even after this incident, the quarrels and fights continued. And she continued to call the police on me, accusing me of having an affair with her husband. On weekends, my mother and stepfather entertained friends. They would spend the night talking, drinking and smoking cigarettes. Then, after the friends left, they fought with each other during their drunken stupor, even in front of the children. It was very frustrating for me, being in that hostile environment. I became afraid of the weekends because I started to get the brunt of her unhappiness. Things got physical—she punched me one night as she continued to accuse me of ruining her marriage.

One day, as she was cursing me, she said: "Look at you—twenty years old and no kids. When I was twenty, I had you already. You should be out there having kids." She made me feel worthless and, no matter what I did, she would always hate me.

One day, she approached me with some money in her hand—one hundred in all. She stretched out her hand to me and said: "If my husband did anything to you, I want you to tell me."

I stared at the money, then at her. I knew my mother; if I gave her any excuse, she would use it to kick me out of the house. Was this money taxi fare out of her home? Where did she expect me to go? I knew what I had to do. "No," I said, "he didn't touch me."

She stood there, watching me closely. Then she lowered her hand, pulled a ten-dollar bill out and pressed the rest into my hand. It was the first time my mother had offered me money while I was with her.

The weather began to get cooler in Montreal and Mother had to buy jackets and sweaters for the little ones. Soon everyone was decked out in winter gear and I still had nothing. One day, my mother took me to a store that had racks after racks of clothing for men, women, and children. They were of a variety of sizes, colors and textures. There seemed to be no sense of organization in the place. There were shoes and boots in one section, some of which seemed scuffed or out of style. My nose began to tickle from the dust.

Mother sorted through a rack that had winter coats until she came to a long, greenish one. She pulled it from the rack and we headed for the cashier where she paid for the purchase. At home, I tried on the coat. The shade of green was dark and dreary, and the material was heavy and felt like upholstery material. Each time I moved, it scraped my skin. I hated that coat, but there was nothing I could do about it—this was what Mother had bought for me so I had to either wear it or freeze. I also knew it was her way of appeasing me—deep down inside she knew how difficult my life was at the hands of her and her husband.

Over time, the strain of living with my mother became almost too great to bear. I became withdrawn and quiet, trying to stay out of trouble, not wanting to draw her anger. It was very easy to spark her rage. One day, in the midst of one of our usual fights, my mother dug her fingernails hard into my breast that she drew blood. That was the last straw.

I ran into the kitchen and grabbed the knife. I rushed out with it, my chest heaving with my anger and frustration. Mother stared, eyes wide, clearly wondering what I was going to do. I thrust it at her. She backed away, watching me warily.

"Here!" I yelled, "Take it!"

She kept watching, not moving, confusion and fear plain on her face.

"Here!" I screamed. "I want you to take this knife and kill me. Kill me now."

She did not move.

"Take the knife," I said again. "F-ing kill me."

I had had enough. I wanted my mother to plunge the knife into my chest and end it all. **On that day, I was ready to die.**

I guess she saw that I was at the end of my rope, because the fighting ceased right there for that day. It was then that I decided I had to leave my mother's house.

When her husband got home from work that evening, I begged him to send me back home to Jamaica. I could not see myself living there anymore. He must have seen my frustration. That same week, he and I went to purchase my airline ticket back to Jamaica. On February 5, 1977, only four months after arriving in Montreal, I was on a flight back home.

## IX

After I got back to Jamaica, I found out that Fitzroy was in the hospital. When I eventually got the chance to visit him, my heart cringed at the sight of him lying there riddle with pain. It was then when I decided to become a nurse to take care for Fitzroy if he ever became ill again.

I stayed at Aunt Joyce's house in Kingston for a short while and then I went to the country to Miss Clem's house. I did not stay at my grandmother's, but I went and visit her. I was afraid of Uncle Beb's promised. I did not feel safe at Momma's place—I still felt he could break the door down at any time and beat me.

After staying with Miss Clem for a while, I went back to Kingston and again stayed with Aunt Joyce. I was constantly questioned by friends and family. "Why did you leave?" my relatives asked. "Why didn't you stay in Canada and get a job?" I was going on twenty, so I could have gone on my own, they said. All of this made me stop and think. Maybe they were right. Maybe I should have stayed and tried to make my way. Had I wasted my opportunity?

In spite of all my fears of being in the same house with my mother, I decided I had to try again. I sat down and wrote my stepfather a letter. I do not remember everything I wrote, but I do remember promising: "I'll be good." He would know what that meant. He would get what he wanted without a fight—that was exactly what I wanted him to believe. I just wanted him to help me back to Canada, and then I would do everything in my power to survive on my own.

It just so happen that my cousin was returning to Canada after being newly married. Therefore, I took that opportunity to ask her to deliver the letter to my stepfather. He paid my way back to Canada. He reopened the door, for me and this time, I was going to take full advantage of the opportunity.

In May of 1977, I came back to Canada with a plan. I was apprehensive about coming back to the hell I had fled, but I knew there was nothing for me back in Jamaica—I had to make a life in Canada. I immediately went job-hunting. By July, I got a job working for a pharmaceutical company. When I got my first paycheck, I eagerly headed home and offered my mother some money. I was glad to be able to contribute to the household expenses. But she refused to take anything from me—she looked at my outstretched hand then turned and walked away.

By this time, the harassment had started again, but I tried my best to stand firm against the advances of my stepfather. He was always trying to grope me or he would try to pull me onto his lap. I continued to fight him off, and so he never succeeded in his fondling progressing to anything further.

I tried to keep myself as busy as possible, so I could stay out of his way. By October, I started evening classes at Montreal High

School, studying French, English and math. I also started to go to church and began to have less and less to do with the home. But that caused another problem—whenever I would go to church, my stepfather would say that the pastor wanted to sleep with me. I did not let it faze me. By this time, I was twenty years old and determined to chart the course of my own life, regardless of what was going on around me.

I started taking the children to church with me, but their mother and father put a stop to that. I ended up going to church alone on Sundays. Even then, the bickering with my mother continued. I thought that, upon my return to Canada, things would improve. They did not—just like before, Mother seemed to need no excuse to start a fight.

Then a different problem faced me. One night, when I got home from class at around ten-thirty, I found the front door locked. I knocked and knocked but no one would let me in. I could hear my sisters and brothers inside the apartment crying, "Let sister in, let sister in." But my mother told them to shut up and sent them to their rooms. I kept on knocking for a long time, but still she would not let me in—not even her husband would come to open the door for me.

The October night was cold, and I worried how I would manage outside in the frigid temperatures. I walked to the back of the building and climbed up the fire escape to the back door of the apartment—they had locked this door as well. With nowhere else to go, I slid down to the floor of the fire escape, wrapped my arms around myself and stared off into the dark night.

I crouched back against the wall, praying that no one would see me hiding on the fire escape. From time to time, I heard sirens and my heart would race. *Had someone seen me? Had they reported me to the police? Would I be arrested?* I was confused and afraid.

Eventually, despite the bone-chilling cold, I must have drifted off to sleep. I awoke to the click of the lock on the back door—Mother had finally unlocked the door. Cramped and in pain, I slowly got up from my crouched position and gingerly pulled the door open and entered the kitchen. My mother was preparing her breakfast and the lunch she would take to work, behaving as if nothing had happened. I did not say anything to her. I went straight to my room, changed my clothes, and waited for her to leave for work. It was only then that I went into the kitchen and began to prepare breakfast for the children.

The next time I had to go to evening class, I did dress in warmer clothing just in case Mother decided to lock me out again in the cold. Good thing I did, because I had to seek refuge on the fire escape again. The only time I was allowed into the house was at 5:30 a.m., when my mother was leaving for work.

Each time I went to evening class, which was held twice a week, I would end up spending the night outside. A couple of times I walked a few miles to my cousins apartment, but I could not do that too often because they were newly married and she and her husband, Chappy, only had a one-bedroom apartment. It was Chappy who offered me a sheet and pillow while I slept on the couch. He always made me feel welcome and comfortable by offering me refreshments, as for my cousin she always went off to bed. I did not want to become a burden to them, so I continued to hide on the fire escape at night, but as time passed and the nights got colder, I began to fret. What would happen to me when the snow started?

Finally, in late November, sick with worry that I would one night freeze to death, I confided in one of my co-workers.

"I'm having such a hard time at home," I started, then hesitated as she looked across the lunch table at me.

She must have seen something in my face, something that told her to prod me for more information. She gave me a look of concern: "What's wrong, Myrtle?"

"I'm trying to go to school," I started, and then stopped as a sob rose in my throat. My eyes burned; I tried my best not to cry, but the tears gathered as I spoke. "I'm trying to get an education . . . by going to evening classes, but every night when I get home my mother locks me out of the apartment. I have to sleep outside on the fire escape." The tears were flowing freely now. I struggled to swallow the lump in my throat, to hide my pain, but it was as if a dam inside me had burst and the tears kept coming. The pain was too much to hold inside.

She was shocked to hear what my own mother was doing to me. One day, while I was at home, that co-worker showed up at our building. She pulled up downstairs in her car, tooted her horn and called for me to come downstairs.

As soon as I went to her she said: "Listen, Myrtle, I'm getting you out of here."

I was speechless. Finally, I blurted: "Where will I go?"

"Don't worry about it," she said. "You're working. You can rent somewhere. I have a friend who has a room available. You can stay there."

She got out of the car, some big black garbage bags in her hand. She had come prepared. She walked with me up to the apartment.

"Get all your things together," she said. "You won't have to spend one more night in this place."

She stepped boldly into the apartment and, although my mother was right there, she did not show one ounce of fear. I took her to the bedroom that I shared with my sisters. She began to take my clothes off the hangers.

"Put all your clothes in these bags," she said, "everything."

A feeling of gratitude flowed through my body. I could not believe this woman was doing this for me. I knew so few people in Montreal and now I was getting the help I needed to move on. I did not hesitate. Within minutes everything I had in my mother's place was packed into the garbage bags. When Mother came to the door to see what we were doing, I did not look at her. This time I did not shiver in fright, my friend was with me and she gave all the strength I needed.

That day, I walked out of my mother's house—out of the house where I had suffered physical abuse and sexual harassment—and into a new life of independence and dignity.

## X

The person from whom I rented the room was a big help to me. She talked to me about the Canadian way of life and how to survive in this society. She also showed me a bit of Canadian cooking. I remember when my landlady put the house key into my hand; I stood there for a while, almost in disbelief. For the first time in Canada, I had a key to my home—it was a great feeling to finally be independent.

After some time of living on my own, I became more confident and moved on to get a self-contained, one-bedroom apartment with a living room and kitchen. Now that I was on my own, I started to receive quite a few invites to parties, most of which I turned down, but if I did go I made sure I was home before midnight. One particular party I attended, I did not know many of the people there, but recognized a few. One of them was a young man who had asked me out a few times. I believe my mother and his mother were co-workers. That night he approached me again seeming full of confidence. I hoped he was not going to ask me out on a date, I wished he would just take no for an answer.

This time there was a slight smile on his lips, but it was not a pleasant smile. "I hear that you are sleeping with your stepfather."

I stared at him, horrified. "What did you say?" I whispered.

"You're sleeping with your stepfather." This time he said it louder, as if to include everybody else in the conversation.

I looked around and yes, people were staring at us—at me. Even the ones with their backs turned to me as they chatted turned to stare; including the ones on the dance floor—all of them seemed to have heard his words.

"It's a lie," I said fiercely. "It's nothing but a lie."

The boy flashed his phony smiled at me, shook his head and then walked away.

After that, I could not stay at the party. It seemed that everybody was watching me and whispering about me. I left that night, tears streaming down my face as I walked home, feeling sick at heart. My reputation had been tarnished for something for which I was not guilty.

As I thought about it, my conclusion was that Mother had been slandering me at her workplace. The boy must have heard the story from his mother and now he was spreading the lies to others. My heart sank; for it was then I realized no matter how good I was Mother could always find a way to hurt me, even when she was not around.

I got a new job, which was going all right. Also, with my newfound privacy, the communication between Fitzroy and I became much more frequent. We wrote each other and then started talking on the phone.

Our feelings for each other grew stronger until things came to the point where we began to discuss marriage. I loved Fitzroy and I was eager for him to be in Canada with me. I missed him so much and was always thinking about him. I had met several men who wanted to date me—some even wanted serious relationships—but I refused every one of them. I only wanted to be with my boyfriend of four years.

After some discussion, Fitzroy and I decided to get married. He was having a hard time in Jamaica and I was here in Canada, lonely and in need of help as well. So, I went to Jamaica, with the intentions of marring Fitzroy and bringing him to Canada so we could be together.

Financially, I was unable to afford a wedding, but Jean—a good friend of mine—offered to cosign a loan for me at the bank. With the money, I would be able to cover the costs of the wedding.

I arrived in Jamaica in late January 1979 and the wedding took place on February 2, 1979. It was a private ceremony, nothing grand, but to me it was beautiful. That was a very happy day in my life. I wore a long wedding dress and we went to the church and got married. Even though no one from my family was there, I was happy, and beaming with joy and pride. I returned to Canada two weeks later, a married woman.

While the immigration papers were being process for his stay in Canada, I took the opportunity to furnish the one-bedroom apartment for his arrival, by financing the living and dining room set in hopes of us working together to pay it off after all it would be our first home as a married couple.

During this time, Fitzroy and I stayed in constant communication. Each time, when there was an appointment for him to see immigration, he would let me know. After five and a half months of waiting, he called to say he received his visa—with that I sent him an airline ticket.

In preparing for Fitzroy's arrival, I arranged with Phillip to accompany me to pick-up Fitzroy from the airport. Phillip was a friend of Chappy's, whom he introduced to me before he left for Miami—If I needed help I could ask him. Because Chappy was aware of the treatment I received from my mother, and that I was on my own, he figured that I might need a big brother as he was to me.

When I met Fitzroy at the airport, I was simply overjoyed. I would finally be able to make a life with the man I loved and we would be there for each other. I would not be lonely anymore, I thought. After returning home from the airport, we all sat down to enjoy a wonderful meal I had prepared for my husband's arrival and, as such, Phillip thought it was a perfect moment to take some pictures. Fitzroy and I ended the evening cuddled in each other's arms.

After spending the weekend together as husband and wife, laughing and reminiscing about our past all too soon, it was Monday morning and time for me to return to work. My days could not go fast enough with work and school, because all I wanted to do was get home to be with Fitzroy, where we would, on occasion, entertain friends or just relax and watch television.

The emotional aspect at the time was great, but financially it was beginning to take a toll on me. So it was a relief when Fitzroy decided to find a job, which did not take very long for him to do.

With his newfound job, I thought we were well on our way to financial stability and paying off some of our debts.

Fitzroy was not a stranger to my friends and extended family and even to some of the tenants in our apartment building. At times, he would visit a friend who lived above us and, often times, a few of my female friends would visit when I was not at home.

At first I thought nothing of it, but after a while, I began to suspect he was making passes at them—I always known his reputation of being a ladies' man. Fitzroy would call the girl in our building and they would talk on the phone and sometimes he would find an excuse to go up to see her at her apartment. I was very uncomfortable with his behaviour.

Then I started to receive mail from Jamaica for him. At first, I would just pass them to him, but when I noticed he was receiving a lot of mail from one particular person—I got curious. I opened one of the letters and that was how I found out he was corresponding with a woman in Jamaica, telling her to apply for her passport and, in return, she was thanking him for the money he had sent her. I realized it was the pocket money I was giving Fitzroy, because at the time the letter was dated, he was not working. I knew at that point I had made a big mistake in marrying him.

Not only did I love Fitzroy, but I also loved his family, whom I have taken as my own, especially his mother, Miss Clem. After reading the letters, they made me so upset, that I wanted to kick Fitzroy out of my home and my life. But I felt I owed his mother some explanation, because I was the only person, in a way, responsible for him. I ended up mailing off all the letters to his mother so she could read them and see the problem I was already having with him.

After reading the letters from his mistress in Jamaica, the relationship between Fitzroy and I was never the same. It shattered the dream that I had for our life together. I could not sleep at nights and I would get up at about midnight and walk the block, in the dark, all alone. I felt like I was going crazy. Then there were the arguments—Fitzroy and I would get into frequent fights. "Where are you going in the nights?" he would keep asking. "Are you seeing someone?" However, there was no one; only myself, going crazy over Fitzroy and his betrayal.

A few weeks later, Miss Clem wrote back to me, voicing her disappointment with our situation. She encouraged me to be strong and try to work out our differences as best we could. She concluded the letter by telling she loves us and will be praying for us to have a good life together.

During this time, Fitzroy was working, but I wondered if he took it seriously. When it rained or the weather changed, he would not go to work. Even though he was working and collecting his paycheck every week, he would not assist me with buying groceries or paying any bills—he gave me nothing towards the maintenance of our home. I could not understand why he was being so stingy. This was not the thoughtful and generous Fitzroy I knew and fell in love with.

One evening, while at work, the frustration hit me and I came home fed up. I went straight into the bathroom where he was taking a shower. "Fitzroy," I said, "if you weren't here, I would not be looking to you for help, but now that you are here, I expect you to help me." I paused just long enough for the words to sink in, then I added: "And if you don't want to help me, then I want you to leave."

I guess the word leave must have hit home—I do not think he was expecting me to say that. He probably thought I would never use those words, because I was so in love with him. In my opinion, he was saving his money to move out on his own accord.

Fitzroy slid open the shower door and stood there before me, stark naked. I could see his body turn red. His face darkened in a frown. "Do you want me to leave?"

"Yes," I said, staring back at him, refusing to be intimidated.

"Do you really want me to leave?" His voice was cold, but his glare told me he was angry.

"Yes."

There. I had said the word. I had done it. But, in truth, I was saying yes from my mouth, but not from my heart. I could not have said anything else. I said yes but deep down, I wanted him to meet me halfway. I wanted him to say, *"Okay, Myrtle, I will start pulling my weight"*. I really wanted our relationship to work.

I stood waiting, hoping to hear those words from his mouth. However, he said nothing. Without another word, Fitzroy got out of the shower, dried off and went to the bedroom. He dressed quickly, and then headed for the bedroom door. I rushed forward, putting my body between him and the door, trying to block him, to keep him from leaving, but he just pushed me out of the way and left.

Distraught and frustrated, I watched as Fitzroy walked out of my life. The fact was I still loved him. For a long time I stood there by the door, still not believing what had just happened. I closed my eyes, trying hard not to burst into tears. After a while, I took a deep breath and walked over to the telephone. After what had just happened, I could not stay in the apartment that night—I needed to be around friends and people who cared about me to get my mind off what had just happened. I dialed the phone number of my friend Erda.

Within minutes of my call, Erda and her husband came over to get me. Grateful to be in the company of friends, I got into their car. They drove me to the grocery store to pick up a few items and then they took me to their home in LaSalle. I was in no rush to go back home to my empty apartment, so I accepted Erda's offer and spent the rest of the night, as well as the weekend at their place.

I was grateful for the few days I spent at Erda's place, because I was able to gather my thoughts and make a decision in moving on. After returning home, a few days later, he came to the apartment and we attempted to reconcile. But it didn't work, so he got the rest of his things and left.

For days, I was in denial—I could not believe he could walk out just like that. We met again and tried to work out our differences, but nothing came of that either. Finally, we came to the mutual agreement that it would be best for both of us to go our separate ways.

As Fitzroy's sponsor to Canada, I was responsible for him for a minimum of ten years. Because he was no longer in my care,

I had to advise the immigration department of our break-up. Fitzroy was allowed to stay in the country, but he was restricted from sponsoring anyone until the ten-year period was over. At least that meant he could not use me as just a stepping stone to get a woman to Canada. It was a small consolation for losing my first love—the man with whom I thought I was going to spend the rest of my life.

After Fitzroy, left I worked hard, struggling to keep up with the loan and other bills, but it was no use. I kept falling behind in the payments—with two incomes that would have been possible, but my meager wages could not dig me out of this financial mess. In the end, I concluded that filing for bankruptcy was my only option.

Even though I had filed for bankruptcy, I did not realize the bank would go after my cosigner, Jean. I contacted her and assured her that I would still pay off the loan. I knew if I did not honour the loan, it would have had a negative impact on her. So, I was determined to clear that debt no matter how I did it. She was relieved to hear this. I was true to my word—little by little, I made payments against the loan, until finally after one year I could tell her that it had all been cleared.

My next step was to file for a divorce—which process took about a year and a half. After that, Fitzroy was a free man—I was single again, a little more mature and, I hoped, a little wiser.

I gradually got my life back in order, surviving on my own as I had done before. I found a job at a factory and was grateful for the small, but steady income. I was lonely, living alone in my apartment, so I began conversing with my cousin Monica who I grew up with in Momma's house, telling her of all the problems I was going through. During one of our conversations, I asked her if she was interested in coming to Canada for a vacation and she said yes. I sent her an invitation letter and soon after that, she came up from Jamaica to join me in Montreal. She spent a few months with me, and then she moved on.

Back at my job, I continued to work hard, keeping myself busy. I was not into parties and drinking, so I hardly went out. Eventually, I found someone—a pen pal I was corresponding with from Jamaica who used to send me beautiful cards that described his love in rich detail. Dean's cards would tell me exactly what love was all about. He was so romantic and I felt like we were beginning to fall in love after corresponding for a year.

One day on a Saturday, around midday, I was at home when there was a tap at my door. I opened to see a man standing in the doorway. I gasped—it was my pen pal, Dean. It was the same man I had seen in the photographs he had sent from Jamaica—about five feet ten inches tall, he was lean with low cut hair and clean shaven face. He wore a button down shirt and slacks. In the photos, he had looked a lot cuter, but I could see that it was him. He looked very decent.

"Dean . . . how did you get here?" I asked. The question must have sounded ungracious, but I was too shocked to be polite.

According to what he told me he had come to Montreal, found a job, worked two weeks, and then had gone out and bought me a ring. He got my address from the envelopes I had mailed to him.

Now he was here at my apartment and he was asking me to marry him. I stared back at him in disbelief. How could I even think of marrying a man I barely knew, except for the letters we had exchanged? He looked at me eagerly. Obviously, he was ready for marriage, but I was not. "I'm sorry," I told him. "I can't." I had to send him away that day—disappointed.

On a subsequent visit to Jamaica, I decided to call on Dean.

"Did you come to see me?" he asked

"No, I didn't come to Jamaica to see you," I responded honestly. "I came down on other business."

I could see that he felt hurt by what I had said. It seemed that I was always hurting him, but none of it was intentional. I just did not want to lie to him. In spite of everything, he still tried to contact me after I returned to Montreal. In the end, I had to admit that I did not have that sort of interest in him, so I just let the communication falter and die. Later, much later, I tried to find him on another trip to Jamaica but to no avail. I never heard from him again.

Years later, as soon as the restriction on Fitzroy was lifted, the first person he sent for was his mother. I am happy about that, even though he and I no longer had a relationship. Having Miss Clem in Canada would be like having a mother of my own—She is the mother I never had.

Miss Clem once said to me "You are my first daughter-in-law, and you will always be the first. Nobody can change that." Miss Clem, my adopted mother, will always be very special to me.

I have always thought that, had we been living in Jamaica, Fitzroy and I would still be married today. We would have had his family as a strong source of support I knew I had the love of his family, even though some in my own family rejected the idea. They felt that because Fitzroy married me, and then left so soon after, he had only used me to come to Canada. They did not think he had good intentions.

For my part, I would say that in a way, they might have been right. Fitzroy may have seen marriage to me as an opportunity to come out of a small community that had little to offer a young person. On the other hand, I felt that I needed him in my life at that time—his presence, his companionship, his love. I thought that, instead of each of us suffering and struggling while apart, together we could make each other stronger. Unfortunately, it did not work out. We were both young maybe it was not the right time. I hold no grudges for what happened between us.

## XI

In spite of this newfound stability in my life, one question was always on my mind: Who was my real father?

"Charles is your father," I often remember my grandmother saying.

I remember time after time when Charles visited Jamaica, Momma would go out by the road to greet him and I would be right there, at the tail of her dress.

"Charles, this is your child, you know," Momma would say to him.

He would just laugh. He never said anything, neither agreeing nor denying. He just looked at me and laughed. I remembered those incidents and I decided that one day I would be the one asking him those questions.

In 1981, I flew to Jamaica to visit Charles's family. They gave me his address in England. After I returned to Canada, I got in touch with Charles's son Lloyd. We both corresponded for a while, and then I decided to go to England for a visit.

When I arrived in England, my cousin Dell and her husband Les met me at the airport and I stayed with them for some time. I also visited my aunt Winnie for a few days and then I went on to spend some time at Lloyd's home. While I was at his home, he spoke about his father.

"When you meet him," he said, "he's going to take you to a room and sit you down and talk with you."

Lloyd made Charles seem like such a serious man that I began to feel apprehensive. I thought about what kind of person he was. My thoughts were constantly on our upcoming meeting. However, despite my concern, I was determined that whenever I did meet Charles, I would get my point across. I planned to tell him exactly why I was there.

Finally, the day of our meeting arrived and I was informed that he was a pastor. Charles greeted me warmly. He was fair skinned and tall. I could see the beauty of his personality shining through as he smiled at me. Well dressed in his suit and tie, he was a handsome man, and he embodied an air of humbleness that made me comfortable in his presence.

He brought me into his office, "Now, Blossom," he said, sitting up in his chair, "tell me what this is all about."

"Well," I said, also sitting up straight, "I've always been told that you are my father, so now I want to know from you." I looked him straight in the eye. "I left Canada and came all the way here for your answer. Are you my father?"

After a lengthy conversation, I came to terms with myself that I may never know who my father is. I guessed he must have noticed my demeanor because he got up from behind his desk, came over to where I was and said: "Blossom, I accept you as my daughter, but I cannot tell you that I am your father—your mother would have to tell you. She would have to answer that for you." He took my hand and I stood up to face him. He gave me a hug. "I do accept you as my daughter," he said again, and I could see in his eyes that he truly meant it.

I spent the evening with Charles, talking to him, getting to know him. He wanted me to meet the rest of the family, so I waited with him and his wife and some of the children until the others got home. Later, one of the daughters came in through the front door and I heard her voice clearly: "Okay, where is this person who is supposed to be my sister? Where is she?"

She walked into the house and came over to me. I stood up to greet her. She took one look at me and stepped back. "Oh my God, she's my sister," she exclaimed. "She looks like us."

She stared openly at me, "Oh, my God," she said again, "she looks just like me. Look at her freckles. She's one of us."

Most of them had freckles. They were so beautiful. I had suddenly found myself among a family that looked just like me.

That night I stayed for dinner and had a wonderful time getting to know Charles's family. Charles's wife was very kind. She catered to me, making sure that I had all I wanted to eat. The children were so friendly and loving that I felt right at home with them. There were thirteen children in the family. I did not get a chance to meet all of them. But for those that I did meet, they showed me nothing but love.

The following day, I went back to spend time with them, and was fortunate to be able to spend a third day with them before I was to return to London. While in London, I was able to do a lot of sightseeing. On different occasions, my cousins would take turns showing me the beautiful sights of London, such as the changing of the guards at Buckingham palace and the renowned London Bridge. My stay in England would not have been complete without taking a ride on one of the fastest trains called the Eurostar International Passenger Train. It was so exhilarating to be able to get from one stop to the next in a matter of minutes.

The day before my departure to Canada, Charles, his wife and entire family came to visit me in London. I was overwhelmed with emotions and gratitude, cherishing the time I spent with him, wrapped in the embrace of his loving family.

Nevertheless, therein lay my dilemma. What about the family in Jamaica, of the man whose name I have? My mother had given me the name of Aris already. How could I abandon that side and take Charles's name and family as my own?

"Don't worry about finding a new family," Aunt Winnie told me. "Just settle for the family whose name you have. You are Myrtle Adalsa Morrison and that's it."

What she said made sense, but still I struggled because I had grown to love my new found family, even in that short space of time.

My vacation was over; I left England and returned to Canada feeling refreshed and happy. It had felt good to be the centre of attention. Even the people at work with whom I shared my experiences were happy to hear about my family. I hoped to maintain a relationship with them, even from a distance.

Re-adjusting to life in Canada after a month long visit to England posed a bit of a challenge, because I had gotten used to the idea of having company around. So, I decided to go to the movies with a friend later that evening. After I got home from work, I was relaxing while watching television and drifted off to sleep. Suddenly, I jerked out of my sleep. I do not know what woke me but I knew immediately that I was not alone—someone was in my apartment.

I peered into the darkness and saw the hazy shadow of a figure tiptoeing around the room. As I stared, the figure moved from one door to another, checking the coat closet, the broom closet and opening the door to the bedroom. *Was he making sure I was the only one in the apartment?* I thought. He must have seen me lying on the couch, fast asleep. *What was he planning to do?*

My heart pounded in my chest and the fright threatened to stifle me. I could not lay still. I jerked upright. "What are you doing in here?" I asked. "How did you get in?"

The man jumped. He whirled around and rushed towards me, pulling a dagger from a sheath at his side. "Shut up!" he yelled. "Where is the money?

I responded by asking: "what money"? I started to screamed. I yelled, "Help! Rape! Thief!"

"I do not want to rape you. I just want the money," the intruder yelled.

He raised his hand and the knife sparkled in the dim light. While still sitting in the couch, I grabbed his wrist with both of my hands. A surge of strength rushed through me and I held onto his arm, refusing to let go. I was a slim girl of only ninety-four pounds and this was almost seventy pounds heavier. I do not know where

I got the courage or strength, but I struggled with this man, alone in the apartment.

I screamed. "Help! Thief!"

*Dear God, please let somebody come to help me*, I prayed, even as I struggled with the man standing over me.

Suddenly, I knocked the knife out of his hands. I lunged and grabbed it, then whirled to face him. With one blow, he knocked the knife out of my hand and it went sailing out of sight. Before I could move, the man rushed at me and began punching, smashing his fist into my body and face. Then, he grabbed me around my neck, trying to choke the life out of me. I gasped, struggling for air, and threw myself off the sofa, dragging him down with me—only then did I break his hold.

My shin burned from where it had been rubbed raw on the fabric of the sofa, but I had no time to worry about that—I had to find the knife. I wrenched out of the man's grasp, scrambled to my feet and ran in the dark room towards where I thought the knife had fallen. Frantically, I felt around, I could find nothing. I jumped up in time to see the man rise from the floor, knife in hand. However, I was determined to live, so I grabbed his arm again and held on all the while screaming, "Help! Help! Thief!"

We fought for a long time and I kept fighting for my life. Finally, he pulled his arm out of my grasp, turned and ran out the back door with the knife still clutched in his hand.

I watched him rush through the door. I hurried to lock it behind him, afterwards I ran out the front door and down the stairs to the floor below. I pounded on the door of one of my neighbour's, a girl I had recently met. As soon as she opened, I went in, breathing hard, still frightened.

"A man . . ." I gasped, " . . . a man just broke into my apartment."

"What?" Her eyes widened, as she looked me up and down, taking in my disheveled appearance. "Come; sit here before you fall down."

She pulled me over to the couch and as I blurted out the details, she reached for the phone.

It seemed that the police arrived almost immediately. I was giving them my statement, when I began to notice a burning sensation on my head. I placed my hand on my scalp and to my horror, it came away covered in blood. From the base of my hand to the tips of my fingers, I was dripping with blood. I had not felt any pain during the fight. I had been so focused on staying alive that I did not noticed that I had been wounded—the knife had sliced my scalp and I did not even realized.

"Do you want to go to the hospital?" one of the police officers asked me.

"No," I said, still so frightened that I was shaking. The thought of going to the hospital scared me. "I have a friend," I said. "Can you take me to her house?" They did, promising that they would be in touch with me soon.

After that, I could not stay in the apartment. Each time I entered the building, I had vivid memories of the attack—the fright, the struggle, the knife coming towards me. I felt like I was being watched wherever I went. I just did not feel safe anymore.

I went back to get some clothes for work and that was when I saw the marks on the bedroom window as if someone had been trying to break in. I did not remember seeing those marks before. Another time when I went to the apartment, the mesh on the window had been cut open and the window was open. I had to make yet another report to the police.

Within days, I found another apartment and was out of there for good. Fortunately, I had a considerate friend in my life at the time, Tony. He would sometimes come over and keep me company, so I would not have to be alone. He brought his guitar and played music until I drifted off to sleep. "Night Nurse" by Gregory Isaacs was one of his favorite songs he used to play for me. Tony was good therapy during that traumatic time. Thankfully, he was there when I needed someone.

Two weeks after the incident, the police sent a limousine to pick me up from work to attend an identification line. I looked at all the men in the line, but no one looked familiar. The police called me three times after that for the ID line up, but I was never able to identify the perpetrator. The police stated that they believed my attacker was connected to some other incidents, which had occurred in the neighborhood. I could not clearly recall all his features because everything happened so fast when I woke up that night. In the end, I had to tell them that I could not help.

Meanwhile, I continued to have serious problems at my work place where I was working as a packer. I had made a lot of friends and the management was good to me. The owner of the company was so friendly that at lunchtime, he would often come and sit at the table with my co-workers and I. He would even pick food from our plates and eat with us. Eventually, this caused friction with some of the other employees who seemed to be jealous of his attention towards us—that, I could live with, but the real problem started with my supervisor. I was friendly with two women on the work floor and he must have thought I was gossiping about him to them. I later found out that he liked both women and that might have explained why he was so suspicious about me.

He made my life a living hell. If I left to go the washroom, within a minute he would be knocking on the door. If I was out of his sight for any period of time, he would start asking around for me. He watched my every move and yet, he did not behave this way with anyone else. He was constantly watching me, until I felt like I could not turn without having him at my back.

When I had taken vacation to go to England, I thought that by the time I returned things would have settled down. Instead, they got worse. The nagging continued and escalated. Even during the traumatic period following the break-in, he continued to nag me. This went on for some time until one day things reached a boiling point. I had had enough. This time when he tried to push me around, I threw caution out the window and stood up to him in front of everybody.

"F*** off!" I shouted.

The packing area staff froze, they were shocked at my outburst—and so was I. It was never my intention to use such foul language and I could not believe I had actually said this to my supervisor. I was immediately ashamed.

Still, I did not apologize—he deserved it. I marched off without looking back, grabbed a card and punched it out. I was surprised when I saw that it was mine because usually I would spend a minute or two looking for it before I found it. I left work that day, not knowing what I was going to do next.

Soon after I got home, the telephone rang—it was the owner of the company. "Myrtle, will you come back to the office?" he asked. "I'd like to have a talk with you."

I went to see him the following day.

"You're a good worker," he said. "I want you to return to work."

I sighed and shook my head. "I'm only a worker," I said. "It is easier to replace me than to replace a supervisor. There is no way I'm coming back here for him to be my supervisor so I think it's best if I go."

The manager looked concerned. "But if you quit, you will not receive unemployment benefits. Are you sure this is what you want?"

"Yes," I said, resigned to my fate.

"Okay," he said. "You will receive your record of employment in a few weeks."

We parted, and I was sorry to lose such a pleasant boss, but I knew there was no place for me there as long as that supervisor remained.

As the manager had stated, my record of employment arrived in the mail and in the space "reason for leaving" it said: "shortage of work". Nowhere did it state that I had quit. This was a thoughtful move on the part of the manager because this meant I would be entitled to unemployment benefits. I breathed a sigh of relief.

Now, with no job, I had to rethink my situation. The break-in was still fresh in my mind. I was terrified to stay in my apartment and even in the city of Montreal. I decided that this was a good time to move to another city.

I wanted to move to Toronto, but I was unfamiliar with that city, or did not know anyone living there. I wrote to the *Toronto Star*, asking for information on a place to stay. They sent me the information but, before I could start making contacts, I received an unexpected phone call from my cousin Monica—She was in Toronto. I was happy to hear from her and I told her of my intention to move there. She invited me to stay with her. I was so grateful. I immediately made plans to move. It was 1983, I was twenty-six years old, and I was ready to start my new life.

# The Toronto Years

# XII

I arrived in Toronto in February of 1983, soon after; Monica introduced me to the agency she worked for, which placed people in health care positions. Although I did not have the qualifications that were required for the position, I was still employed by the agency. While working, I went back to school and successfully completed the Health Care Aide program and received a certificate. The move to Toronto was a positive step in my life.

My relationship with Tony did not last because of the distance. He came to Toronto a few times, but eventually our connection dissolved. Monica and her friend Marsha introduced me to a life that was very different from what I was accustomed to—Wednesdays to Sundays we would go night clubbing.

One night, Marsha visited the condo and, as usual, we all got dressed, helped one another with make—up and then we were ready to go. Monica was a great fan of skirts and dresses and tonight she did not disappoint. With her full breasts and narrow waistline, dresses were the perfect complement to her curves.

Marsha was more conservative, wearing black pants and a top. Being Chinese, she had straight jet-black hair that she had cut short in a bob just above her ears, giving her a boyish look. At about five feet and six inches, she was the tallest of the three of us.

That night I dressed in a Wayne Clark two-piece suit, which consisted of blue satin pants that blended with the light blue multicolor silk blouse. I had paid a lot of money for the suit and each time I wore it, both men and women would comment on how beautiful I looked. We headed out with Marsha, the city of Toronto was waiting for us and we were only too willing to oblige. From nightclub to nightclub we went, first to Carib, then to Cutties. We passed through a club at Victoria Park and another on Finch Avenue, and so we went on for the night, sampling each nightclub then moving on.

At our final stop for the night, we got a table and sat down to relax with drinks. As the room pulsed to the rhythm of a slow song, I slowly sipped my virgin Strawberry Daiquiri, enjoying the feel of the cool liquid sliding down my throat. I was humming the tune, "Stealing love on the side", when I felt someone tap me on the shoulder. I turned to see a tall smiling face man reaching out his hand as if to take mine—he wanted to dance. I smiled but shook my head. I was not in the mood to dance just then. He did not insist, just shrugged and walked away.

I went back to sipping my drink and enjoying the music, but I was disturbed three more times. Whenever a new song started someone else would come over to ask me to dance. I kept turning them down, but with a smile to take the edge off my rejection. By this time, Monica and Marsha had found partners and were enjoying the music on the dance floor. I was still nursing my drink.

Although it was not an alcoholic drink, normally, I drank so little that one glass could last me all night. I was happy to sit there, relaxed and looking at couples on the dance floor.

I was startled when a man slipped into the empty seat beside me. He had low cut hair and a straight face and he was smiling at me. The other men, who had come over to ask for a dance, had been polite enough to remain standing, but this one was invading my space. I wondered how he could be so bold.

The man leaned towards me so that I could hear him above the nightclub noise. "I've been watching you, I notice that a lot of guys came over to ask you to dance," he said into my ear.

I looked at him and raised my eyebrows but said nothing.

He leaned in again: "I'm going to ask you for a dance and I don't want you to say no."

I opened my mouth to say just that but he stopped me.

"Come on, just like I was watching you, people are looking at us right now. Don't embarrass me in front of them." He gave me a pleading, puppy dog look. "Just one dance. Please?"

I looked at him, shook my head and smiled. Then I gave him a nod. What else could I do? How could I say no when he asked like that?

When I went out on the dance floor, I did not regret my decision. They were playing one of my favorite songs, Percy Sledge's "When a Man Loves a Woman." When that song was playing, I had to dance. That night I left the club with Monica and Marsha exhausted but happy.

Through my contact with Monica, I met a man who was in the United States Air Force. His name was Stanley. He was about six feet tall and around a hundred and eighty pounds—he was a big guy from what I saw and he had a pleasant personality.

Stanley and I began talking around April of 1983, and eventually started a friendship that blossomed over time into a relationship. However, it was a long distance relationship because he was always travelling around the world. During the first year of our relationship, Stanley travelled between the USA and Canada, coming to see me as often as he could. We had some good times together during those visits. He took me out to restaurants and we went to parties. He even offered to drive me to Montreal to see my mother and the rest of the family. I thought that now we might be able to build a relationship as mother and daughter.

Stanley had one of those cars that had no separation between the front driver and passenger seats. Throughout the journey, he had me sit there beside him with my head on his shoulder. I fell asleep and woke up again with my head resting there. When we arrived in Montreal, we went straight to my mother's house, where I greeted my brothers and sisters happily. Initially, when I had just left, I was not allowed to visit or see the children. Whenever I would send gifts for the children, Mother would throw them out—she even threw away money I had given them. This time, however, it was all right. I felt more comfortable with my mother. Stanley and I spent the night at her house. We returned to Toronto the next day, where Stanley and I enjoyed a few more days together before he headed back to work.

One of my most exciting memories of my time spent with Stanley was our trip to Niagara Falls, where we did the bus tour, the boat ride and, best of all, the helicopter ride. I cherished the memories of those wonderful times together. They comforted me when Stanley was called to service and deployed overseas with the U.S. Air Force. He had to travel to distant countries, so I knew his visits would be few and far between. At those times, all I had were my memories.

Easter of 1984 came around and I decided to go to Jamaica to visit my grandmother. Momma was always in my thoughts. I was particularly concerned because I had heard that she had suffered two strokes. I just had to see her.

I called my good friend Penny in Montreal and asked if she would like to go to Jamaica with me. She agreed and I happily began to make plans. I was glad that Penny would be going with me—we always did things together. Penny was beautiful with her dark skin, pert nose and curvy body. She wore her shiny black hair straight and at shoulder length, and she always looked fashionable with her face perfectly made up and her signature burgundy lipstick on her lips. I, on the other hand, was of lighter complexion with a slim body; we were the perfect complement for each other.

Penny and I headed to Jamaica for our two-week visit. We did not stay over in Kingston, but instead went straight to the house in the country. When I saw my grandmother, my beloved Momma, my heart wept. The woman who had raised me since I was three months old—a woman I knew as always being vivacious and active—was now lying in bed, unable to move without help.

Momma had always been a jovial person, always smiling and cheerful. She enjoyed life, and it seemed that, to her, the best part was being a Christian. She used to read her Bible aloud, sing songs from her sankey book and pray long and loud. She had such a beautiful voice; I loved listening to her sing those hymns. Moreover, when she prayed she would ask God to bless everyone, including the enemies. To see her now, wet and needing to be changed often, made me weep.

Many years before, Momma predicted that her daughter Icema would be the one who would be there for her to the end—she said this to me many times. And so it was, although it must have been a difficult decision. Aunt Icema left her home in Kingston and moved to the country to take care of her mother. This role of caretaker must have been rough and even frustrating at times. I was extremely grateful to my aunt for the sacrifice she made to ensure that Momma lived her last years in dignity.

As I sat at my grandmother's bedside, talking to her and holding her hand, my mind flashed back to the times when she would be up and about in her yard among her vegetables or cooking or cleaning the house. My memories of her were of a vibrant and energetic woman. Her current reality was very different—I mourned all that she had lost.

Still holding her hand, I looked my grandmother straight in the face and asked, "Momma, if you had to make only one wish what would you wish for?"

She paused then a soft smile spread across her lips. "My wish would be to go to Pond side Church and see Minister Powell one more time."

Pond side Bethany Baptist Church was the church she had attended for most of her life. Minister Powell was an integral part of it all. He was renowned near and far as a great preacher and respected in the community, as a dedicated minister to the people. My grandmother's wish was to be part of his congregation one last time.

"Okay," I said, "we will go to church on Sunday."

Momma stared at me, eyes wide and her shock evident. "How am I going to go?" Her voice tinged with sadness and frustration. "I can't even get out of the bed much less up the hill."

"Don't worry about it," I said as I smiled at her. "Just leave everything to me."

When I left my grandmother's side, I went in search of Uncle Beb. I told him about the plan to take Momma to church on Sunday. Being the man he was, I knew he would do everything in his power to make this happen. He immediately took charge of the arrangements for transportation.

Sunday arrived and we all got up early to get Grandma ready for the journey. Dressed in her Sunday finery, Momma looked radiant. Friends and members of the family lifted her and carried her the half mile to the waiting car. We drove through Armstrong, Balaclava and Oxford, then all the way up to Roses Valley. Because of the poor condition of the road, the car had to stop a half-mile or so from the church. The volunteers had to lift Momma again and carry her the rest of the way.

Once inside, my Grandma sat down in the pew and began to cry.

"What's wrong, Momma?" I glanced at her tear-streaked face. "Why are you crying?"

She shook her head, for a moment unable to speak. Then she spoke. "Tears of joy my child," she whispered, "tears of joy for getting this chance to come to church one last time." For her, the unbelievable had come true.

The members of the church were thrilled to see her. Minister Powell came over and greeted her warmly. When Momma became ill, he would sometimes come to the house to pray with her, but still it was nothing like worshipping in the Lord's house. That day Momma, testified how happy she was that her granddaughter Blossom had made it possible for her to attend church today. She thanked everyone for always keeping her in their thoughts and prayers. She thanked her daughter Icema for taking care of her. Finally, she sat down and a look of contentment settled on her face. As I watched while my grandmother listened to the sermon, my heart filled with joy. I was so glad that I made this possible for her. When she got in the spirit, calling on the name of the Lord, I began to cry. But just like Momma, they were tears of joy.

A few days later, I got the chance to visit Kingston with my friend Penny. We met up with Miss Clem's son Ryland, who took us to one of the most beautiful beaches in Jamaica, called Hellshire. We also spent the afternoon shopping for souvenirs. We then returned back to the District of Marlborough to spend some more time with Momma and a quick visit with Miss Clem. Finally, it was time to return to Canada.

That was one of the saddest days of my life. I could not bring myself to leave. I began to cry and so did Momma. I was filled with the fear that, once I left, I would never see my grandmother alive again.

"Come on, Myrtle," Penny pleaded. "We have a plane to catch."

Still I lingered, trying to squeeze in one last moment with my beloved grandmother—I had to go but I did not know how to leave.

"Myrtle, we will miss the flight." Penny pulled at my arm until I could not ignore her any longer.

I reached for my grandmother and hugged her tight, savoring the feel of her in my arms. Finally, I kissed her and told her goodbye. Then I left.

All the way to the airport, one hundred and twenty miles away, I cried. I could not shake the feeling that I was losing Momma forever. She was mother, father and grandmother to me. She had been my strength, my constant fountain of love and kindness. On the plane, the sadness consumed me and, even when I arrived in Canada and returned to work, I could not shake the veil of melancholy. I threw myself into my work, doing double shifts, trying my best to take my mind off my grandmother.

The sight of Momma, reduced to such frailness, had such an impact on me that I immersed myself in the care of others. I went on to a career as a personal support worker. I did not get the chance to take care of my grandmother as I really wanted, because I could not physically be there for her. Instead, I dedicated myself to doing what I could for others like her.

Shortly after my return from Jamaica, I decided to find a place of my own. I had been living with Monica for quite some time, but now I felt I needed a change. The fast-paced life and the night clubbing was a lot of fun, but I was getting tired of that lifestyle. It was not for me.

I rented a room from an Italian lady, where I got settled. I had gotten to know the city of Toronto fairly well because of my nightly adventures with Monica and Marsha. I no longer felt intimidated by its size; I was very comfortable being on my own.

Five months after my visit to Jamaica, I received an unexpected phone call at work—Momma had passed away. The cloud of sadness that had surrounded me for so long swelled and burst. Just as I feared, I would never again see Momma alive. It took me some time to come to terms with Momma's death, but when I finally accepted the news, and my stream of tears slowly dried up, I began to feel a new emotion—a little relief that Momma was not suffering any longer.

I called Stanley to inform him of my grandmother's death. He gave me his condolences and encouragement. Within a few days of the news, I was on a plane back to Jamaica. My relatives in Jamaica were surprised that I had come for the funeral, seeing that I had been there just a few months earlier. But I knew why I was there—I could not let Momma go into the ground without saying my goodbye.

Many family members from overseas had also journeyed to Jamaica for the funeral—my mother was one of them. I think many of my relatives were surprised because I was so attentive to her during the journey to Marlborough. They knew the history of my relationship with Mother, so they did not expect this of me. She was not feeling well so, despite our past, I did my best to make her feel comfortable. I bore no grudges against her.

Although Momma's funeral was a sad occasion, it also brought many family members together from across Jamaica and overseas. I greeted relatives I had not seen in years—it was nice seeing them.

The day of the funeral was sunny and bright. It was as if, like us, nature was celebrating my grandmother's life. So many people attended the funeral—from Marlborough and the surrounding districts—I felt proud that Momma was so loved and respected by the community.

After the funeral, I stayed a week at my grandma's house—the home that I had known as a child. This place held so many memories for me, good memories of my grandmother when she was strong. I remembered the stories she used to tell, the laughter we shared, and the love she always gave in abundance. As the memories flooded back and the tears flowed, I still smiled because, from my grandmother, I had learned to love, really love.

On my return to Canada, I began to work even harder, holding down three jobs at one time. This was what I needed to keep my mind off Momma. I was torn between wanting to keep her buried in my heart and wanting to feel her presence every day. I found myself wearing her nightgown to bed almost every night and I dreamt about her constantly. I would wash and iron her nightgown every week and stick my nose in the clothes steamy from the iron, just to get a whiff of Momma's aroma rising from the armpit of the gown.

I also moved to a new home. After holding down three jobs, I was more than able to afford a place of my own. While I was looking for a place to rent, another tenant from the apartment I was renting was also looking. Lilieth and I decided that we should rent a place together. We rented the top floor of a house; it had two bedrooms and an eat-in kitchen. It was very cozy, my roommate and I got along well together. Eventually, we converted the dining room into a third bedroom for another roommate. We all shared the bills and lived comfortably together.

In October of 1985, Stanley came to visit and gave me a surprise. We were in the bedroom getting ready to go out when Stanley took out a tiny box, opened it and presented me with two gold rings. "Myrtle, will you marry me?" he asked.

Surprised and touched by the gesture, I looked at him, but said nothing. I could not speak for a moment as I thought about what it would be like to be married to him. Then I thought about the fact that he was always away. How many times would I have to be alone when he had to travel because of his career in the Air Force? Would he be there when I needed him most? When I lost Momma, he had not been there for me—I had to deal with my grief all by myself. I looked at the two gold rings he had brought me, each of them so thin, like two pieces of gold wire lying in the box. *Does he really love me?* I thought.

With all these questions racing through my mind I slowly shook my head. "No, Stanley," I said softly, "I can't accept your proposal."

Stanley stared at me with disappointment plain on his face. For a moment, there was silence then he said: "Why don't you think about it?"

We finished dressing and drove downtown just as we had planned. We did not bring up the proposal, but it weighed heavily on both our minds. When we got back home, it was time for Stanley to bid me goodbye.

"It's not over," he said, as he hugged me tight. Then he picked up his bags and hurried out to his car. Three months later, I found out, I was pregnant.

I was happy about the pregnancy because, at the age of twenty-nine, I was the only one among my friends who did not have any children. In the early period of the pregnancy, I continued to work hard in the nursing home. There, I had to do heavy lifting such as using the Hoyer lifts to take clients off and on beds. I also pushed the residents in wheel chairs to various areas within the facility, among other duties. Eventually it began to take a toll on me.

As the pregnancy progressed, my doctor prescribed bed rest for me. The day before Christmas, I decided to go to see Pat, my hairdresser. The walk to the salon was only a few blocks, but my stomach felt heavy so I held it while walking slowly. When I arrived, I told Pat how I was feeling.

"I'll do your hair quickly," she said, "then you can go home and get some rest. And if you need a break, just let me know."

I nodded and sat back in the chair so she could get started on my hair. After a while, I felt like I needed to use the bathroom. "Give me a minute," I told Pat, and headed down the stairs to the washroom.

I was easing myself onto the toilet when I saw blood. Something was wrong with me. I was passing blood.

"Pat!" I screamed. "Pat, come quick."

Within seconds, she was running down the stairs and bursting into the washroom "What is it, Myrtle? Are you okay?"

She saw the blood and panicked. "Oh, my God," she screeched. She rushed in to help me. Then she ran back upstairs and dialed 911.

"Oh, no," I said, as I leaned against the sink. "I've lost the baby."

When the ambulance arrived, I was a nervous wreck—it was as if a shot of electricity was surging through my body, causing my nerves to be on end. I was shaking and shivering with uncontrollable tremors, to the point where the paramedics were holding down my legs to keep me still. Soon after, I was rushed to the hospital. There it was, confirmed by the paramedics that I was having a miscarriage. I was admitted to the hospital where they performed a dilation and curettage (D&C) and I had to stay overnight. A D&C is a surgical procedure that opens up the cervix and removes the excess contents of the uterus from a miscarriage. My roommate at the time, Lileith, was considerate enough to bring me an overnight bag, knowing that I disliked being in the hospital and wearing the gowns provided.

I was released the following afternoon, which was Christmas Day, supposedly the merriest day of the year, but I was in despair. I had really wanted that baby. Could I even have one? What was wrong with me? As I sat at home, alone, lost in my thoughts, there was a buzz at the door. To my surprise, it was Aunt Joyce and my cousin Monica visiting. During their visit, I informed them of my miscarriage—they hugged me and comforted me. I was so grateful for their presence. For that evening, at least, my relatives helped to take my mind off my troubles.

Later that evening, I called Stanley. I told him about the pregnancy and the subsequent miscarriage. He gave me words of comfort, but even as I spoke to him, I knew that I was not destined to have a future with him. His work took him away for such long periods of time—I realized he could never be there for me. Already, he was not there when I had to deal with the pain of my grandmother's death and he was not here for me now at the loss of our child. Stanley and I spoke several times after that. I told him how depressed I was, with so much going on in my life.

I remembered, expressing to him: "You're never around."

Finally, I decided to be totally honest with Stanley. "I can't go on like this. You cannot be there for me the way I need you to be. It is over, Stanley. I need to start anew."

Stanley did not accept this news very well. He always seemed to maintain the hope that we would be together. He continued to call me whenever he got the chance. Still, things were never again the same between us.

I rested for a week or two and then returned to work. I continued to push myself, trying to forget my double loss. When the Easter holiday came, I got a welcome change when my brothers and sisters came to visit. I was so happy to see them—I took them shopping and bought lots of things for them. When I put my brothers and sisters on the bus back to Montreal, they were laden with groceries and gifts. To me, it was money well spent.

I felt that I needed a break. I wanted to leave Canada for a while, so I decided to go to the States. I needed to be in a different environment, to renew myself and come back refreshed. I discussed my plan with my roommate and decided to go our separate ways. I gave up the place where I was staying and stored my furniture at Prudence's house. My sister Martha from Montreal decided to join me on the trip. Over the course of time, Martha and I kept in constant communication by letters, even after I moved from Montreal to Toronto. Martha would always complain how miserable she was living with her parents. They were separated and she was living with her mother, but went back and forth between the two parents. So, when she asked me if she could accompany me to the States, I did not have the heart to say no. I had to reorganize my trip to assume the responsibilities of my younger sister.

On our way to the States by bus, we encountered some difficulties at the border for having too much luggage. The immigration officer took one look at our big bags and shook his head. "The only thing missing are your pots and pans and kitchen sink."

He opened my sister's luggage, rummaging through it, when he came upon her photo album. He took it out and started flipping through the pages. Then he frowned. "What's this you wrote here? I am Martha and I am here to stay. This is not just a visit, is it? You plan to stay here for good."

"No, sir," I piped up, "that's not what she meant."

But it was no use. We were put on the next bus back to Toronto.

I had already given up my apartment, so when we were sent back, I stayed with my friend Prudence, with whom I had met during our health care aid-training program at Centennial College back in 1984. She allowed me to stay with her and her family for a while until it was convenient for me to try to cross the border again. I decided, next time I was going to try the train. We waited two weeks before trying to cross the border again, this time we did not have any bulky luggages and we successfully crossed.

In the USA, we went to the Bronx and stayed with Aunt Emma—the same aunt I used to live with in Kingston. She was very excited to see us, especially me, because the last time she had seen me I was a teenager. When I saw her, I remembered the days in Kingston. I had so many good memories, but I put the bad memories behind me because I appreciated how Aunt welcomed us into her home and showed us love. She seemed so happy to have us there with her.

While staying with Aunt Emma, I met a gentleman, a correctional officer, who lived just across the street from her house. He was very tall, about six foot three, and quite handsome.

Whenever we happened to pass each other outside, we always greeted one another. One day, while we were talking, he asked where I was from. When I told him, he seemed a bit fascinated that my sister and I were Canadians. Marvin and I became good friends. We did not really go out, but we spent a lot of time at his house in the Bronx. Eventually, our friendship developed into a relationship.

Marvin and I started to spend more time together. Martha would frequently join us, because she was bored staying home. However, Marvin grew weary of me always bringing her along. On one occasion, when I went to visit him, he had a friend that he introduced to my sister and me, for the sole purpose of distracting her. The idea of a stranger, wanting to take my sister out, did not sit well with me, because I did not know the individual to entrust with the wellbeing and safety of my sister. I was outnumbered because my sister was eager to go out and Marvin encouraging the idea. In the end, all I could do was ask my sister, to be back by 11p.m. "Martha", I said, "If you go out, you need to come back at a certain time because we are staying with Auntie and we don't want her to kick us out."

That night, 11 p.m. came and there was no sign of Martha. Then at midnight, still no Martha. I kept sticking my head out the window, looking for her. Two more hours passed and still no Martha in sight. I ended up getting the flu from sticking my head out the window all night. But how could I go to bed not knowing where she was. Finally, at about 6 a.m., a long black car pulled up in front of the house, like a stretch limousine, and out stepped Martha. I was so angry I did not call out to her; I did not even go down to open the door—I went straight to bed.

After a while, she no longer kept to her curfews and began coming home later and later. My sister used to listen to me when she was in Canada, but in the USA, she changed. Maybe it was because she saw the way my aunt's grandchildren related to their grandmother—they never listened to her. Perhaps it was because, whenever I said one thing to Martha, my aunt would tell her the next.

When I said to Martha, "You're not going out," my aunt would pipe up: "This is my house so if she wants to go out, she can go."

With such support, Martha found the courage to curse me out in front of our aunt, making fun of my freckled face. To hear those words from my own sister was hurtful. This trip was supposed to be a time to refresh my mind and body after the trauma of losing my baby and grandmother in one year. I felt betrayed by my sister, who ruined my trip. Her behavior even brought back a lot of hurtful memories from my school days in Jamaica.

I later found out that Aunt Emma was calling Mother in Montreal to report on Martha and me. Everything we did, everywhere we went, Mother was told about it. There was no privacy.

At this point, I felt that we should leave Aunt Emma's house. It was becoming too uncomfortable to stay with her. Then, to make matters worse, she started putting restrictions on the use of her telephone—even to make a local call to our cousin became a problem. More than that, she tried to turn my sister against me, encouraging her to be defiant towards me. The respect that Martha had had for me in Canada was gone.

After Martha overheard a conversation between our aunt and mother, it was then that she realized that Aunt Emma was not as forthcoming as she had thought. She apologized to me and we decided to leave our aunt's home because we felt if we stayed any longer, she would have succeeded in ruining the relationship between us.

We left Aunt Emma's house and went to stay with Uncle Enos in Upstate New York. He was happy to see us because his relatives hardly visited him. He showed us off to all his in-laws and friends in the area, saying he was so proud of his beautiful nieces. We settled at our uncle's place and, because my money was running out, I decided to find a job. I was successful in doing so and started working. My sister, on the other hand, complained that she was stuck in a room all day, while our uncle and I were out at work. I was so caught up in finding a job to take care of us; it did not cross my mind my nineteen-year-old sister could be working as well.

As it turned out, my uncle's wife was not very nice to us. It was obvious that she did not want us there. She had never accepted my uncle's side of the family, so when we showed up, she was uncomfortable having us there. She would fix the meals, call our Uncle to the table, and then Uncle would call my sister and I. After sitting at the table my uncle would ask, "where is the girl's breakfast"? His wife would say, "I did not make any for them". Uncle would try to share the breakfast from his plate, but I said no, and made our own. In the evening, my uncle's wife would watch

Jeopardy on the television. When that was finished she would turn off the lights and television, and go to her room, leaving us sitting in a dark living room.

One night, Uncle Eons came home from work and saw us sitting there, no light no TV. "What is wrong girls?" he asked. "What are you girls doing, sitting in the dark?"

When we told him that his wife had turned off the television and all the lights and had gone to bed, he got angry and marched into their bedroom slammed open the door, stomping his feet. "Don't you ever do that again!" he shouted. He then swore at her, walked off in the direction where we were and then he turned on the television. "This is my family," he declared, "and they can watch the TV if they want to." After this incident, we never had that problem with her again.

My grandmother would oftentimes tell me stories about Uncle Enos when he was a young man; how strong he was. Although he was not a person to start a fight, if confronted he could defend himself at any cost and always ended up being the winner. My uncle was also my grandmother's defender from her husband. There were instances when my grandfather wanted to beat on Momma, but had to take a step back when Uncle Enos was around.

Still, I did not want to cause a rift between my uncle and his wife, so after just a few weeks, we moved back to the Bronx. This time we stayed with my cousins Pamela and Michelle.

Not long after our arrival at Michelle's home, I noticed that Martha was eating a lot, sleeping more puking on occasion. I also noticed the sudden growth in her breast, which in my opinion, were the classic signs of pregnancy. It was then I confronted Martha with my observation. I consulted with my cousin Michelle and she suggested that we contact the young man and have Martha take a home pregnancy test. After contacting her male friend, we went to the pharmacy and did the test—Martha was pregnant and the young man was encouraging her to have an abortion. He then turned to me and explained: "Myrtle, I grew up without a father. It was very difficult for my mother; therefore, if I'm going to have a child I want to be there for that child. Since Martha will be going back to Canada, the best thing for her to do is to have an abortion."

Upon hearing his statement, Michelle was confused and I was furious, because the situation I was trying to prevent from happening was staring me in the face. Turning to me, visibly distressed, Martha asked me: "Blossom what do you think I should do?"

I stared at her, too angry to even speak. I had tried so hard to watch out for my younger sister, trying to get her to understand the importance of abiding by her curfew, trying to keep her out of trouble. She had defied all my guidelines and now she was asking me whether to have an abortion. I shook my head. "You know what? You're going back to Montreal to your mother. I don't want any part of this." I sent Martha back to Montreal, where she would have to face motherhood and I did not think she was ready.

I felt at ease once Martha was back with her parents. At this point, I decided to spend a little more time at Michelle's home and continued my relationship with Marvin. As time progressed, I noticed strange, but familiar changes taking place in my body. I was sleeping a lot, eating more and craving for things I wouldn't normally eat, such as hamburgers, hot dogs, and steamed cucumbers. I also found myself gaining weight, which I did not think was anything much to worry about, seeing that I was only 90 pounds.—gaining a few more pounds was a desirable change and one that I embraced.

The following morning, while lying on my side, I opened my eyes and there staring back at me were two eyes. Thinking I'm imagining things, in disbelief, I closed my eyes and reopened them again—to my horror I saw my grandmother lying beside me staring at me. I screamed, jumped over the sleeping bodies of my cousins and off the bed.

"What? What's wrong?"

My cousin jerked upright from where she had been sleeping on the bed. She looked around wildly.

"It's Momma," I stuttered. "I just saw her looking at me. I just saw those eyes."

Pamela looked at me as if I had gone crazy. But I knew what I had seen and I knew Momma was trying to tell me something. I decided to take a home pregnancy test, which indeed confirmed that I was pregnant.

I called Marvin and asked him if we could meet. When we did, I told him I was pregnant. Seeing that I was carrying his child, he asked,

"Do you want me to marry you?"

"No," I responded quickly, feeling a twinge of annoyance. From the speed with which he had thrown out the question and from the tone of his voice, I knew he wasn't being genuine—this was definitely not a proposal. In fact, I noticed a hint of sarcasm. What did he think; I wanted him to marry me so that I could stay in the States? I was insulted and wanted no such thing from Marvin.

The fact was I probably would not have married Marvin even if he had truly meant it. I had come to realize that he was not the one for me. From his actions, I could see that he was not a very generous person. He was just too uptight, even with minor things. Instead of shopping at the grocery store and getting all that was needed at one time, he would go out several times a day and buy just what he needed for a particular meal. It was very strange to me, so different from how I did things. I knew I could not be with a man who did not plan for the future.

A few weeks later, I returned to Toronto. There I stayed with my friend Prudence until I found a place of my own. I ended up renting a room from a former co-worker. I was fortunate enough to land a job with my previous agency, this time working from home. I was a dispatch coordinator for health care workers. I was happy with that job, because I was embarrassed to be seen in public with my growing belly. I phoned my cousin Michelle in the Bronx and mentioned how I felt cooped up in the house. I told her how I sometimes felt lonely and depressed. Coming back from the USA to Canada, pregnant and with few friends, sometimes my situation got to me. She decided to introduce me to her child's father who lived in Toronto. "You can call him. He'll be a good friend to you," she told me. "He's a very caring person. I'll touch base with him so he'll expect your call."

Later that day I rang the number that my cousin had given me. "Hello, may I speak to Terry?" I said.

"This is Terry," the voice answered. "I've been expecting your call."

The first thing that Terry asked was if he could assist me with anything—I assumed Michelle told him about my situation. I could tell she was right about him; he was kind-hearted. Not long into our conversation we realized that he owned a unisex beauty salon just across the street from my building.

"You're joking," I said in disbelief. "I'm going out onto my balcony. You step outside and I will tell you if I can see you."

I went out onto the balcony and, there he was, standing just across the road with the phone in hand at his ear. He waved and I waved back.

"What's your apartment number?" he asked.

When I told him he came right up. When we met, it was like meeting an old friend. He was full of laughter, a happy, easy-going man. He made me feel so comfortable around him. There were many things that I wanted to talk to him about, even then on our first meeting, but I decided to hold back and only talk about my stay in the States. He was a good listener. I just wanted to open up and tell him about my ordeal, but there was something telling me, *not yet*.

When he was ready to go, I thanked him for coming over. "I'm glad I met you," I said—and I meant it. "Remember, I'm just across the road."

"Tomorrow, I'll come get you and take you for a drive. I can see how depressing it can be for you. You need to go out." Terry seemed genuinely concerned.

Next day he was true to his word. We went for a drive and then ended up at a coffee shop, where we chatted and got to know each other better.

"I've been over to your salon so many times and had no idea who the owner was," I said, smiling. "Now, when I go to Terry's Beauty Lounge I can say I know Terry personally."

From that day on, we continued to keep in touch. I was happy to know that Terry was part of my family. He was such a nice person, someone I could call on if I wanted to talk or if I needed help. He was always helpful—he took me out to dinner and parties just to get me out of the house. He knew I was afraid to be out on my own being six months pregnant, he became a very dear friend and has remained so throughout the years.

A few weeks before Allicia was born, I was pleasantly surprised to receive a letter from Aris' son Tyrone. He wrote that he had heard a lot about me from his father and that he would like to get to know me. He mentioned he was a supervisor at the Jamaica Railway Corporation in Kingston. He enclosed his telephone number, so I could get in touch with him whenever I visited Jamaica again.

I continued to receive letters from Tyrone on a regular basis—it was a pleasure corresponding with my newfound brother.

As time passed, and it got closer and closer to my delivery date, I began to get anxious. I was eager to have the baby. My due date—May 18—came and went and still there were no signs that the baby was ready to come. I had no contractions at all.

"Don't worry," the doctor said. "It's fine to have a baby two weeks before the delivery date or up to two weeks after."

When I entered my third week passed the due date, I was very concerned. I went back to the doctor for my weekly visit.

The doctor informed me my baby's head was not engaged. "If the position does not change in a few days you need to get to the hospital," he said.

For the past few times I had gone to see my doctor, there was another lady who happened to be there on the same day—we must have been given the same appointment. When she heard that I was now going three weeks overdue, she said, "Myrtle, you are going to have this baby tonight."

"Really?" I was skeptical. The baby had not shown any interest in coming out before. Why should it come tonight?

"I am going to make you laugh until you have that baby," she said.

That night She, Terry and I went to the movies to see *Beverly Hills Cop*, starring Eddie Murphy. It was hilarious. I laughed so hard I thought I would have the baby right there in the cinema. I actually started to feel cramps.

When I got home, I took a shower and began to get ready for bed. Before I settled down, my friend Lilieth called to check up on me at 11p.m., as she did every night throughout my pregnancy during the evening news cast. After we spoke, I went to bed and, about two hours later, the pain started again. I tried to bear it for as long as I could, but it kept getting worse and I could not sleep because of the pain shooting through my body. Finally, I called Pat, my hairdresser and friend.

She said without hesitation: "You're in labour. You need to go to the hospital right away" she said.

I took her advice and immediately called a cab. At this point, I was petrified of going through labour by myself, because I did not know what to expect. Even though Terry and I had become good friends, I did not feel that I could bother him at that hour of the night. I headed out on my own. As soon as I arrived at the hospital, I was checked into the room, where I spent the night writhing in pain. The following morning my doctor came to see me. "I'll have to induce labor," he said.

Throughout the day, the pain got worse. I moaned and shifted in the bed, trying to find a comfortable position, but I was hooked up to a monitor so I could not move freely. I lay there, alone in the hospital, with no one to rub my aching back or even hold my hand. I groaned my pain aloud, but there was no one to hear me.

Finally, an anesthesiologist came and went over the procedure for administering an epidural. I curled into a ball with my perturbing stomach in front of me as they inserted a needle into my spine. This position was very uncomfortable as I tried not to jerk my body during the procedure as contractions continued. But at this point I would have done anything to get rid of this excruciating pain. After twenty-two hours of labour pains and no baby, the doctor came back and told me it was time for him to do something else.

"Myrtle, if you can't get something through the door, won't you try to get it through the window?" he said.

I nodded, confused, and said, "I trust you, doctor. Go ahead and do what you have to do."

I was quickly prepared, wheeled off to an operating room for the emergency procedure. I was having a Caesarean section at 10 p.m. they pumped more painkillers into me and then began. I will never forget that experience—I was awake for the operation and they kept speaking to me, informing me of each step they were taking.

"Ok Ms. Morrison, I'm going to pass my finger along you stomach, let me know if you can feel anything."

"Do you feel anything?"

'No," I replied

"Scalpel!" He shouted to the nurse.

"Ms. Morrison we'll be making the incision now."

"Okay." I said as I heard someone ask for a basin.

"You'll be feeling a tug, but not to worry". I did feel a tug, but there was no pain. They took the baby out but it did not make a sound. After a few seconds, I heard the cry and the doctor informed me that I had a plump baby girl, weighing nine pounds and six ounces. I heard everything in the operating room, from the directions given to the nurses to the doctor reassuring and keeping me aware of every move he was making. When I heard that glorious sound of cry from my precious baby girl, I knew exactly then she was finally brought into my world.

My little girl was rushed to the intensive care unit to be placed in an incubator. To my utter dismay, I was told that she swallowed some fluid and also developed jaundice.

After, I was wheeled into my room; I later got up to go to the bathroom. I don't know why I thought I was able to get there by myself, but I did. In that moment, I realized that my legs were not my own—I was like a baby trying to walk for the first time. I couldn't feel the lower half of my body from my abdomen to my toes. I held on to the edge of the bed for dear life, fearing for the worst—the reopening of the incision from the surgery I had a few hours ago. I was really scared and, in that moment, I knew I had made a terrible mistake. I should have stayed in bed and called a nurse to assist me. I don't know if it was one of the other patients whom I were sharing the room with who signaled for a nurse, but I was relieved when a nurse walked right in. I was chastised for attempting to do this on my own, because the risk of reopening my wound could have jeopardized my recovery.

I did not see my baby until the following day—I was so anxious to see her. Gingerly, I got out of bed and slowly walked down to the nursery. It took me a long time to get there; I could not move quickly following my surgery. The baby lay quietly in her incubator. I then put on a pair of gloves that were attached to the incubator and, stroked her body gently. They'd told me she was the biggest baby born that night in the hospital.—I was a proud mother.

My baby and I spent a total of nine days in the hospital during our recovery process. I was discharged with a sense of relief knowing that a healthcare provider would be coming by the apartment to assist me as I was still in a lot of pain following the surgery. I gratefully accepted this assistance for three months and then I was on my own to take care of my first child, Allicia.

During my pregnancy, Allicia's dad, Marvin, and I kept in touch. I felt the need to update him on the progress of my pregnancy, which I thought was an important aspect for my unborn child in the hopes that a relationship between father and child would one day ensue. At this point, by July, I made another change—I decided to move from my friend's apartment to be on my own.

By September, Marvin came to visit his daughter, Allicia. He was very excited to see her and proud to be a father.

"She resembles my family," Marvin said, beaming as he held her.

From the time, I told him about my pregnancy until this point—he had made no attempt to offer any support, financial or otherwise. I soon came to realize he did not plan to contribute in any way. I was a single parent with the full responsibility of raising an infant and I conditioned my mind to accept this.

Not being able to work, I was forced to apply for social assistance support to survive. During this time my brother John left Montreal and came to live with me. I spoke to a friend of mine who found John a job in Toronto. Working from Monday to Friday and then going to Montreal on weekends to see his girlfriend. My other brother Abraham would sometimes visit from Montreal, until he also found a job in Toronto and moved in. Now I was not short of company.

I stayed home with my baby for about nine months, and then I enrolled in a continuing education centre to upgrade my skills. An aspect of the continuing education centre that I really appreciated was being taught how to be assertive. I placed Allicia in childcare so that I could have the time to focus on my studies. After five months of upgrading, I enrolled in a Secretarial Word Processing course. My life was heading in a positive direction.

## XIII

One day, I was in the West End of Toronto shopping with a friend when I wandered into a store. As I entered, the owner greeted me warmly. "Oh, you are perfect for my son," she said, with a broad smile. Surprised, I smiled back and soon we were chatting as if we had known each other before. By the end of the conversation, she had taken my telephone number.

A few days later, I received a call from a gentleman named Troy, stating that he had received my telephone number form his mother.

"I'm not her natural son, but we're very close." he explained. "She treats me just like her own child."

After his initial telephone call, we ended up having conversations that were hours long. We talked a lot about our likes and dislikes, our future endeavours, completing my education and getting a job. We also spoke at lengths about our daughters and about how we wanted to be treated by that special someone. We grew closer after a month of chatting, even though we had never met. One day I decided it was long enough—I needed to see this person I'd been chatting with all this time. It was August, right around the time of the Caribana Festival season, and there was a lot of partying going on in Toronto. I asked to see him—he told me he had visitors at his apartment, but he dropped everything and came right over to see me.

I peered through the peephole when I heard a light knock on the door. It was him and thought to myself *his face missed the boat*—I was disappointed. I hesitated, but opened the door and there he stood with a bunch of red roses in his hand. He was not the tall, dark and handsome man as I'd pictured him to be. I relaxed and gave him a smile—I appreciated his gesture of him bringing me flowers. He seemed like a romantic kind of guy and so I settled, knowing that he was not my type. Furthermore, he and I had spoken so much on the phone; it was as if he was like an old friend. Even if he wasn't what I was expecting, I told myself I could live with it. From that point on, things moved very quickly and we started dating.

For our first date we decided to go for a drive. That evening, I got dressed and went downstairs. I was looking forward to spending time with him. But when I saw his car, my smile disappeared. I stopped walking. There, in front of me, was a clunker of a car, so old that I hardly even wanted to get close to it, let alone to get in it. I shook my head.

"I'm not going out in that car," I told him. "Whenever you get a different car, it will be fine, but I'm sorry. I can't go on the road in that."

A few days later, he called me downstairs and showed me a different car. It was a Buick Century, more up-to-date than the one I'd seen before.

"This car is fine," I told him, relieved that I would be travelling in something that looked decent. He then turned to me and said "you're a feisty Jamaican."

During one of our conversations, he told me that he may have a child back in his country, Dominica.

"Are you supporting her?" I asked.

"No," he said.

I looked away, upset at his response. I knew how hard being a single parent could be and I wondered about his child. How was her mother managing without financial assistance from him? Was the child suffering because of his lack of contribution?

I told him in a calm, but firm voice, "I won't date you unless you start supporting your child."

That same week, he began sending money to support his daughter. I was glad for his decision and that he would be fulfilling his responsibility as a father.

Throughout all this, I was still on social assistance, but I continued with my studies and managed to get good grades. I was working towards my goal and I was pleased when I ended up graduating with honours. While I was seeing Troy I never mentioned that I was on social assistance—I just wanted to quickly get my qualifications, find a job and get my life back in order. However, despite my caution, he did learn of my plight.

One day I asked my other brother Abraham for twenty dollars to get some groceries for the house. He said he did not have any money. "Go ask your man," he told me. This only added to the resentment building toward my brothers. I was not working, yet expected to support myself, my child and two grown men on social assistance. I could not understand how both of my brothers could be working, living rent free in my apartment and not even spending a cent for food. I was expected to house and feed all of us on my meager welfare cheque.

Nonetheless since my brother, John had been living with me for a while and working, I thought I could teach him to be responsible. I asked him to contribute something to help pay the bills. He called our mother right away and told her that I wanted money from him. Mother was livid and told him not to contribute anything and, with that, he flatly refused to make any contribution.

I really needed the extra cash, but there was no way I was going to ask my new gentleman friend, not after I lambasted him for driving a beaten-up car and for being an absentee father. Instead, I went next door and asked my neighbour whom I have known for years and was also a friend to lend me twenty dollars. He gave it to me and was kind enough to tell me that I did not have to repay him. I used it to get the groceries we needed for the week. As usual, my brothers helped themselves to the food that I brought home. I was just happy to have some milk for the baby.

Later that evening, Troy came by, and he and my brother Abraham was talking then they decided to go to a coffee shop. I later found out, for some reason Abraham told him my life story. He even told my boyfriend about the twenty dollars that I had gotten from my neighbor Barry, who is the brother of my best friend Pat. And, worse yet, he revealed to him that I was on social assistance.

When they got back to the apartment, I could see that something was wrong—my boyfriend looked grim.

"Come," he said. "Let's go for a drive."

I went reluctantly because I could see from his expression that this would not be a pleasant ride. He drove straight to the bank and withdrew sixty dollars. He kept twenty dollars and gave me forty.

"Why the hell didn't you tell me you were on welfare?" he yelled. "Why did you hide it from me?" He swore at me and cursed. He put me down so low that if the earth could have opened up and swallowed me, I would have been relieved.

I thought to myself this relationship would soon be over. I did not want this man to tell me how to live my life and raise my family. At that point I had seen a glimpse of his character that I had not seen before. I knew then I could no longer settle for anyone, I deserved more, much more. It was around Easter time, about seven months into our relationship, when I found out I was pregnant. Now, despite my reservations about our relationship, I was expecting his child. At first, he wanted me to have an abortion, but I refused. Then, before I knew what was happening, he had moved himself into my apartment. The constant pressure of school, my work placement, supporting my family and our rocky relationship really got to me. It was unbearable at times—my home became a place of sorrow rather a refuge.

Living with Troy was not easy I found him to be argumentative. Worse, he was quick to raise his hand to me. One thing I used to hate was the way he would press his middle finger against my forehead and shove my head backward. Worst of all, our spats usually ended with him demanding I get an abortion. Over and over he said it, but no matter what he said, I knew I was never going to do that. Despite the fights and the abuse, Troy lived with me throughout the pregnancy. I only found relief of him telling me to have an abortion when I was four to five months pregnant, when the baby started to move in my stomach. He became interested.

I was scheduled for a second C-section on October 3, 1989. On the appointed day, I sent Allicia to stay with her godparents Pat and Oswald while Troy took me to the hospital.

My second child was born that same day, weighing nine pounds and one ounce. Groggy from the operation, I did not see my baby until two days later. Her father was the first one who held Latisha. They bonded with each other during my absence and by the time I was able to see her, it almost seemed as if he had claimed her for himself.

Troy was a proud dad. When we got out of the hospital about seven days later, Troy was there to fulfill his daughter's needs. He was so involved in her care that at one point I felt like he wished I wasn't there so that he could be totally responsible for her. We argued a lot because I felt like Troy wanted to take over my role as mother. It was a crazy thought, but I was not use to seeing such a hands-on father—I was used to doing everything on my own.

We constantly clashed in our parental duties and it lead to many quarrels. To keep the tension at a minimum, we finally worked out a schedule where, Troy ended up taking care of Latisha at different times. When he got home from working on the evening shift, I would rest the first part of the night while he took care of her. After he got home from his day shifts, he would take care of her during the early part of the day and I would take over for the afternoon and evening. The schedule seemed to work well, as Latisha was a night owl—she would sleep all day and stay awake all night.

Three months after I had Latisha, he and I had a serious conversation. I felt he was competing with me, as if he wanted to win a parent-of-the-year award. I often felt he always wanted to undermine me as a mother. He pushed himself to do everything for the baby, not wanting to include me in anything. I reached my final breaking point when I took Latisha to the doctor one day. Once I got back from the appointment, he wanted to be the one to give the medication to her. He got confused as when to give her the medication and we ended up giving her more than what was prescribed by the doctor. I snapped and shouted at him. "If I am giving the medication to Latisha, let me give it. Or if it's you, then go ahead. But we can't both be doing this because we'll mess up." I couldn't help but feel as though he thought I wasn't a fit enough parent to take care of Latisha. I did not know why he was pushing to do everything. I had the time because I wasn't working yet and he had a full work schedule—it just did not make sense to me.

One night he got up and made milk for Latisha. He came out and saw that I had opened the milk, even though he had opened one the night before. We began with our usual bickering, but this time, he lifted his foot and gave me a vicious slap kick on the shoulder. His five toes were printed on my skin. The impact left me in shock for a couple of seconds, as I was afraid something happened to my C-section wound. Initially I was afraid to look down, but then the pain turned my shock into rage. I retaliated by trying to hit him back, have him feel the same burning sensation his feet left on my bare shoulder. This effort became futile, as he used our baby as a shield. Finally, I just left him alone and walked away. All of this over a tin of milk—I didn't even want to think of what he would do to me if more serious domestic issues arose in the future.

I was so stressed out by his behaviour that I decided to get away. I was going to take a vacation and go to Jamaica with the children. I made all the arrangements, but it was not until I picked up the three airline tickets that he came to accept that I was really going.

"Can I go with you?" he asked

I stared at him. He was the reason I was leaving in the first place. I did not want him tagging along. I did not know if he knew that, but I did not respond to prevent another spat.

He kept asking, over and over, nagging me to the point that I finally gave in. "What have I done?" I later lamented. Still, I consoled myself with the fact that, with him there, I would feel safer on our trip and I could use the extra set of hands while travelling with two young children.

I called my ex cousin-in-law Chappy, who lived in Kingston, and asked if he knew of a decent place where we could stay. He recommended the Bob Marley Guest House, and that was where we spent our first week of vacation. We had a good time in the city, visiting the sights in the vicinity of the guest house. The second week we went to the country to visit my relatives there. I decided to take a day out of the week to go with my Aunt Icema to the Canadian Embassy in Kingston—I was trying to sponsor her to come to Canada.

When Troy heard of our plan to go back to Kingston, he immediately handed me his credit card. "Use this to pay for a nice hotel for the night," he said. "That way you and your aunt won't have to travel back late at night—I just want you to be safe."

I accepted the card with a smile, pleased at his thoughtfulness. He could be so caring and protective towards me at times. He would not allow anyone to harm me. He was the type of man who would defend me against anybody. I just could not protect myself from him.

Aunt Icema and I left early next day and headed for the city. Unfortunately, she did not receive a visa that day. Not having a house and land in her name worked against her. We had nothing further to do in the city, so we decided to head back home that same evening.

When we got back to the country it was almost 11 p.m. Troy was surprised and happy to see us, but unfortunately he was battling a fever most of the day. He'd had the children on his hands while he was suffering and now he was only too glad to hand them over to us. I did not realize how he was until I took his hand and felt him shaking uncontrollably with the chills. I quickly took charge of the situation and rubbed him all over with alcohol, gave him medication, lots of fluid and used cold compresses on him. Finally, during the night, the fever broke. By next morning, he was back to his old self.

During my stay in the country, I went to see Miss Clem. I left Uncle Beb and Troy in the house talking. When I returned home from my visit, my ex father-in-law accompanying me with a box of food provisions, it set Troy off in a jealous rage. He would not let me accept any of the food that Miss Clem had packed—yams, sweet potatoes, bammies and sugar cane—he decided that I was not taking any of it, not even one piece. That was when I found out, during my absence, my uncle Beb had told him about my ex in-laws. My family in Jamaica had strong opinions about why the marriage between Fitzroy and I did not work. This would, of course, colour their conversations about Miss Clem and her family. Uncle Beb painted a negative picture of Miss Clem's family and Troy believed it all. He decided he did not want to have anything to do with them. "We don't want anything from them," was his position. And, to my great embarrassment, Miss Clem's husband had to turn around and head back with all the food his wife had so lovingly prepared for me. It was one of the most humiliating moments of my life.

I ended up leaving the country without getting the chance to say goodbye to the woman who had been such a mother to me. She and her family had shown me such love and care—I could never forget it. That was why it hurt so much, I was unable to accept their gifts and show them how much I appreciated their love and kindness.

Back in Kingston, we again settled into the Bob Marley Guest House. While there, we visited Aunt Eunice in Spanish Town, which was just outside of Kingston. In my conversation with her,

I mentioned that Aunt Icema had not been successful in her visa application for Canada.

"Maybe I could try for the visa," Aunt Eunice suggested. I agreed that it would be a good idea.

We were not in a rush to get back to Kingston, so we spent the night right there at Aunt Eunice's house. The following morning after breakfast, we said our goodbyes and went back to the city. A few days later we were on our way back to Canada.

Now that Troy had been fully informed about my life in Jamaica, once we got back to Canada, he took every opportunity to throw all what he learn about my past in my face. The arguments started all over again and became more and more frequent. He even persisted in doing the thing I hated most—shoving my forehead back with his finger.

Despite my troubles at home, I stayed focused on my studies and eventually graduated. Next, I went job hunting. One day, I was walking past the office of the Registrar General when I looked in and saw dozens of envelopes scattered all over the floor. *Why don't they just hire me to clean this up?* I thought. So, I took matters into my own hands and handed my resume at the front desk. A week or so later, I got a call to come in for an interview. There, I told the manager why I applied for a job at that office and convinced him I could do a great job of organizing the place. Soon I started working as a clerk.

My new job gave me so much more independence, my brother Abraham moved back to Montreal and John moved out on his own. Also, by this time, Aunt Eunice was granted a visa and now living with us. She was assisting me with the children.

Sometimes when I was at work, Troy would come to the office with Latisha and Allicia so we could all have lunch together. Once, a male co-worker of mine met him and said: "So you are Myrtle's boyfriend. Now I understand—all this time I've been asking her out, just to go and have lunch, but she would always refuse". That seemed to trigger some sort of alarm in his head. He didn't say much to me about it, but I knew deep inside it was only a matter of time before his jealousy sent him off the edge.

I started to come home late soon after, because the Office of the Registrar General was in transition, it was moving to Thunder Bay. Therefore, there was new technology that we need to learn before we leave as I was going with the company. He always demanded to know exactly where I was on those days I came home late. One particularly Tuesday evening, I came home later than usual. I was exhausted and relieved my aunt was home to handle the children that night—all I wanted to do was relax. After greeting my aunt, the children and Troy, I went into the kitchen and opened the fridge. I noticed there was no milk, so I decided I would walk to the store across the street to purchase a bag. Before I leave the kitchen he began arguing with me about coming home late. I did not answer him. I was not in the mood for a fight. I remained silent to placate I opened the apartment door and walked down to the elevator. I was standing there waiting for it when Troy came out of the apartment and stood behind me.

"You're not going anywhere," he said. "Go back inside."

I did not even get the chance to reply. He grabbed me by the collar and flung me back towards the apartment door. He threw me with such force that I stumbled and fell to the threshold. I got up and tried to head back towards the elevator, but he grabbed me again and threw me to the ground.

Then he started to kick me—I could feel his foot crash against my ribs. I tried to get up, but nothing could stop him from kicking me.

I turned my face towards the apartment and saw Aunt Eunice standing there watching. He was still kicking me and I was still crying—all she did was stand there, watching.

When he finally stopped, I struggled to my feet with pain shooting through my body as I stumbled towards the door. I pushed past my aunt, who still remained silent. I sobbed as I staggered to my room. I just had time to slam the door behind me, but he rushed after me and punched the door so hard that it split in half—he barged into the room like a raging bull. I grabbed for the phone to call the police, but he ran over and ripped the phone from the jack and threw it against the wall.

I dashed out of the room as he chased me, flinging his fists as he ran. I grabbed a beer bottle and whirled to face him, determined to hit him with it if he attacked me again. Almost snorting with anger, he knocked it out of my hand and tried to hit me again. Throughout all this, Aunt Eunice just stood there watching him beating me and she didn't do a thing to stop him. Finally, when it seemed that she was satisfied with his abuse, she said to him: "it's okay . . . that's enough now Troy."

Only then did he stop hitting me. As soon as he did, I ran out of the apartment to seek refuge at Barry's place next door—from there I called his parents told his stepmom what happen and inform her I was calling the police. Within minutes the police arrived and took me to the hospital.

"Nothing's broken," the doctor said, "but your ribs are bruised. You need rest."

My whole body felt battered and abused. After I was finally released from the hospital the police drove me back to Barry's place. They went over to my apartment late that night, where Troy was fast asleep in bed. When he opened the door, he was in his underpants. I could not believe how unconcerned he was about where I was or what was happening to me. The Police told him to get dressed, and then arrested him. After he was taken away, I called his parents and informed them of his arrest.

For days I was traumatized by the abuse I had suffered at his hands. It came as a relief when I was asked to go to Thunder Bay as part of my job with the Office of the Registrar General. Days before we left for my new assignment, I took Aunt Eunice to my doctor. After my doctor gave her a diagnosis, she called me inside and said, "Sit down Myrtle."

She asked me what my relationship was with Eunice. I responded: "She is my Aunt."

"You need to send her back where she came from, because her blood pressure is high beyond measure—she is a walking time bomb."

I thought that leaving the city would be better for her health. I immediately packed up my family and left. Months later, I was called to a court hearing but was unable to return to Toronto to attend. However, I wrote a letter explaining the reason for my absence. I later learned that, because of my absence, the case against Troy was dismissed.

After a while he started calling me in Thunder Bay. He would ask to speak with the children—I did not deny him that. For my part, though, I tried to keep my distance. After a few months, when the project in Thunder Bay ended, I returned to Toronto. Shortly after that Aunt Eunice left for the United States.

Troy started to come by the apartment to visit the kids after returning from Thunder Bay. He started coming over more often and he ended up sleeping over. Before I knew what was happening, I was involved with Troy again.

One day I sat and thought about all the things I'd been through with him. I told myself I did not want any part of this anymore. I built up the courage, packed up all his things and dropped them off at the neighbour's place. I called him and said: "Go to Barry and pick up your stuff. Nothing of yours is in this apartment anymore."

He rushed to my place, pounded on the door and tried to break through it. Allicia, only five years old, came out of the room. "Mummy," she cried, "let Daddy in." Little Latisha, his daughter, started crying, too.

"Keep knocking," I yelled at the door. "The police will come and remove you soon."

He knew that if the police came, he would be in big trouble because he was not supposed to be within a hundred feet of me. He finally gave up and left.

After almost four years of knowing him, and with all that I had gone through, I would never have imagined I would have felt the way I felt after finally ending the relationship. I felt empty and lonely. With him I felt protected from anything that could harm me outside our home, but I came to realize he was the most dangerous thing in my life. I was used to him being around the children and it pained me to think about raising my children without their father at home. I was really missing him and was tempted to call him many times, but I did not. He called several times throughout the day, but sometimes I refused to answer the phone. I knew I could not totally avoid him, though—he was still the father of my child. I called Aunt Icema in Jamaica and told her I wanted her to come to visit me. She applied for another visa and this time she got through. I paid for her airline ticket and, at long last, she arrived in Canada. A week after her arrival, I headed down to Jamaica, leaving her with the children. I had to get away for a while; I desperately needed a change of environment.

In Jamaica, I spent some time with friends and then visited family in the country. Finally, I came to terms with my emotional turmoil.

While I was in Jamaica I met a gentleman named Curtis next door. He had a straight, handsome face and he seemed very pleasant.

"Hi," he said. "Where are you from?"

I told him I was from Canada.

"You're from Canada?"

"Yes." I nodded. "Where are you from?"

"*I'm* from Canada," he said. I was intrigued.

"Where in Canada?" I asked

"Toronto," he replied. "Where in Canada are you from?"

"Toronto," I said. By this time I was laughing.

"Where in Toronto?" he asked.

"Trudell and Danforth."

"Trudell and Danforth? I cross that intersection every day on my way to work."

"Really?"

From that conversation, Curtis and I decided to become friends. He asked for my number and called me two weeks after his return to Canada. From there we stayed in touch, calling each other regularly.

During this time Aunt Icema was a big help to me, taking care of the children as I adjusted to my life without their father. Aunt Bernice, who was now living in the States, stayed in touch with her by writing frequently. I enjoyed getting news about how she was doing—I could still remember how much I had loved her when she visited Jamaica when I was a teenager.

On my last visits to Jamaica, I was introduced to our aunt, Tit, who is Aris's sister. I remember Aunt Tit being a tall, slim and fair-skinned lady, who was very friendly. She shared many stories with me, particularly about Aris being my father. I will never forget the day I received a letter from Tyrone. It was March 25, 1992, a day after my birthday, relating the sad news.

"Sister Myrtle, I have some bad news to tell you. My aunt, Ms. Tit is dead and buried. She died in December and buried in January. Fire came on the place because of short circuit by illegal connection. She escaped the fire but remembering she had money and bankbook inside the house, she returned inside for the money and was trapped. Got burned to the hands and face, she was taken to the hospital where she was admitted and eventually succumbed to her illness."

I barely had time to grieve over the loss of my aunt. I really wanted to get to know her, and would have liked to develop a relationship but could not because of her untimely death. Reading further through the letter was more bad news.

"Our other brother Dane, who was a foreign exchange officer for the Bank of Jamaica, was shot twice by gunmen in January—he was buying US currency for the bank".

The news of these two incidents took a toll on me. Losing a family member and thinking there was a possibility I might lose another made me stressed and deeply depressed.

Tyrone also enclosed the telephone number of one of his sisters who was living in the States. I was happy to get in touch with her. "I'll soon be visiting some relatives in New Jersey," I told her. "I will call you when I get there."

Not long after Aunt Icema had returned to Jamaica, I got a call from Aunt Bernice. She had called to ask me about a letter she had mailed to her sister at my home. In addition to the letter the envelope contained money. I told Aunt Bernice that I had not seen that letter and that Aunt Icema had already left for Jamaica. Still, I promised to look out for it and get it to my aunt once it arrived.

A couple of weeks passed and I forgot all about the letter. If it had arrived it would have jogged my memory. My next recollection of it was when I got a second call from Aunt Bernice.

"Where is the letter that I sent for Icema?" she demanded.

"I haven't seen it yet, Aunt Bernice," I replied. "I will keep looking out for it."

There was a pause then I heard her voice, cold and harsh, over the phone. "You took it.—You took the money."

"What?" I could not believe I was hearing this. Did she think I was a thief? "I didn't take any money. I haven't even seen the letter."

"God told me you took it," she declared. "Yes, you did it."

I sucked in my breath, taken aback shocked at her vehemence. Was this the same aunt I had adored so much? Then the anger rose inside me. "If the God you are serving told you I took your letter with your money, then you are serving the wrong God," I replied.

It was as if my words ignited a fire in Aunt Bernice. She shouted her fury into the phone, reprimanding me for what I had said, accusing me of stealing her money. No matter what I said, she refused to believe my innocence. As far as she was concerned I was a thief and I could not convince her otherwise.

Finally, I broke in. "I'm not going to stay on this phone with you. You can believe whatever you want. I know I am innocent," I protested. With that, I hung up the phone, cutting off her tirade. Fuming, I walked out of the apartment, trying to put Aunt

Bernice out of my mind. I did not need another stress in my life just then.

It was not until another couple of weeks had passed that the situation was finally resolved. The phone rang and when I picked it up it was Aunt Bernice.

"Before you hang up," she said quickly, "just listen to what I have to say."

I was tempted to slam the phone down, but instead I said coldly: ""I'm listening."

There was a pause then a sigh. "I just want you to know that I'm sorry."

"Sorry about what?"

She gave an embarrassed giggle: "I . . . I got the letter back today. The postal code was wrong."

For a moment I was silent. Then I said, "I'm glad you got your money back," and hung up the phone. Aunt Bernice had fallen off the pedestal on which I had placed her—my glorious image of her had been shattered.

I put Aunt Bernice out of my mind and moved on with my life. Over time, Curtis and I became more than just friends. He often gave me beautiful cards and brought me flowers and, on one of my birthdays, he brought me a heart-shaped ice cream cake full of strawberries. The second Curtis was aware of what I liked; he did not hesitate to get it for me. I liked the fact that we could speak like two reasonable adults. Once, when we had an argument, he wrote me a letter apologizing for his behaviour. He was really a romantic person, considerate and charming.

Curtis and I were dating for some time when I found out I was pregnant. At first I was elated, wanting to see the fruit of our love, wanting to know what our child would be like. Then, for some strange reason, I began to hate it whenever he was around me. During the pregnancy I developed strong feelings of resentment towards him. Just looking at him would upset me. I could not understand it. It must have been my hormones. Whatever it was, it resulted in my doing whatever I could to stay away from him during the pregnancy. When it was time for me to go to the hospital to have the baby, even then I did not want to have him around. I sent for my Aunt Icema from Jamaica so as to watch the children for me. I even asked her not to tell him that I'd gone away to the hospital to have the baby.

At the hospital I was prepped for a C-section. On April, 27 1993, my son Tevin was born, weighing seven pounds and thirteen ounces.

After returning home, I received a call from Curtis. That was when I told him I'd had the baby—within minutes he was at the apartment. He was happy to see the baby. Curtis picked up his son Tevin and looked down at him, our cute little bundle of joy, and his face was beaming with pride. I could remember the day he asked if we could name the baby Tevin, after a singer in the States; I was more than happy to grant his wishes.Next, he turned his attention to me. As he held Tevin he smiled at me, then he walked over to the crib and laid the baby gently into it. He came over to me as I stood by the door, concern plain on his face.

"Are you alright?"

I nodded. "I'm just trying to recover from this C-section."

"C-section Did they have to cut you?"

I nodded again.

"I want to see it."

For a moment I hesitated, and then I slowly pushed my thumb into the waistband of my pants and slid it off my belly. Then I lifted my top just high enough for him to see. To my surprise, Curtis knelt down right in front of me. Before I knew what was happening, he lowered his head and kissed my belly, right on the wound from the operation.

"I'm sorry you had to go through it all by yourself," he whispered. "I'm sorry I was not there."

My eyes filled with tears and as I looked up I saw Aunt Icema standing in the kitchen doorway. From her expression I could see that she, too, was touched by his demonstration of concern. Curtis, no matter what, was a true romantic at heart.

After that, Curtis came around often to see his son. He was truly a proud father. When Tevin was a few months old, he picked him up and was rocking him gently back and forth, when he noticed some rashes on the baby's head. He froze.

"Myrtle," he said; his voice cold. "If you don't know how to take care of my son, I will have to take him from you."

I felt like he had shoved a knitting needle deep into my heart. For a moment I said nothing. Then I calmly walked over to the crib. "Come here, Curtis," I said in a quiet voice.

When he approached I spoke again. "Put the baby down," I said, my voice still calm, even pleasant.

As soon as he did, I walked over to the door. "Come here, Curtis," I said again. As soon as he did, I opened the door. "Out," I said. "Out, out, out."

Curtis hesitated as if he thought I was not serious, but then he looked at my face and he saw that I was not joking. He stepped passed me and out the door and I closed it shut behind him. I was furious. The last thing I wanted was another man to challenge my parenting, especially after what Latisha's father put me through.

After that moment, I noticed that Curtis's interest in Tevin began to wane. While he and I were in a relationship he'd been fine, coming around often to see the baby. However, once he realized that I no longer had any intimate interest in him, he stayed away, hardly ever coming to see his child—not even providing any kind of financial support. Whenever I spoke to him about it, he would come up with a measly sum of money.

"What is this?" I would ask sometimes. "After staying away for three years, this is all you can give your son?"

Occasionally, I would go to his workplace and tell him that I needed things for Tevin. Still, I was not depending on him to take care of my son—I was doing that by myself, but as his father he needed to play a part. The few times I was able to get money from him, it helped a bit, but there was no consistency in his contribution. And the fact that I had to be after him to get it was a real turn off—eventually I just left him alone.

I made a trip to the States and gave my sister Rolda a call as promised. She immediately came over to see me in New Jersey—I was very happy to meet her. I said as I gave her a hug that evening we talked for a long while. Even after I returned to Canada, we continued to stay in touch. I invited her to come over and spend the Easter holiday with us—she agreed. But our joyful plans were never materialized. Just before the Easter holiday, I received a phone call from my sister's daughter saying that her mom had suffered a massive heart attack and had passed away.

Her sudden death was a terrible blow. We had just found each other and were getting along so well, for me to lose her in an instant. I attempted to attend the funeral but I missed it, so I ended up paying my respect at her home after the funeral.

I had met her children and others in the family, it was a sad occasion. I had lost a band new relationship; I had lost a sister. I was left to cherish the gift she had given me the first time we met—a bottle of Boucheron perfume. Even after the perfume was finished, I kept the bottle in memory of our brief, yet loving sisterhood. To this day, I still use that brand of perfume, and it is still my favorite fragrance. I wear it in memory of my sister—to me, she was family and the scent reminds me every time I wear it that the love of family is the most important thing.

# A Different World

## XIV

When Tevin was about three years old, I decided to return to school. I attended Centennial College and enrolled in the General Arts and Science program. After completing this I went on to do a two-year correctional worker program at the same institution. During this time, I was having a hard time juggling school, work and the children.

However, I was blessed to have the help of Auntie Olivia who assisted me with my essays. She often tagged along with me to the library and helped me with my research. At times, I had more than fifteen pages of essays to write, she always stayed with me until they were complete. She was such a source of support. My diploma for the correctional worker program was as much the result of Auntie Olivia's efforts as my own.

Auntie Olivia and I were born on the same day in the same year—maybe that's why she and I bonded so well. She was the kind of person who was always there when help was needed. If I fell short on money, she would say: "Myrtle, how much do you need?" Without hesitation, she would make a deposit into my bank account, no questions asked. I was glad when I was able to do the same for her.

I had a job on campus as a security guard while I was doing the correctional worker program. For this job, I had to do my rounds, walking the huge campus all alone at night. I was scared, but did what I had to do to make a living. I worked twelve hour shifts, from noon until twelve on weekends. It was hard finding a baby sitter. The daughter of a friend of mine would come along with me—she was only fifteen years old. I did not want to leave her alone with my children while I was at work, so I would take her and the children with me during my day shifts.

In one of the empty classrooms, I would spread a comforter on the floor and let the children take a nap while I did my rounds. On my break, I served the meal that I had prepared for them to eat. After that they would go outside to play on the campus field where I could watch them.

During this time, I found out that my second child's father was getting close to my sister. He'd started taking Martha and her children out to restaurants. Whenever Latisha happened to meet with her children they would gloat: "Oh, your dad is taking us to MacDonald's," or "Your dad is taking us to Wendy's." Latisha, who was around ten, was greatly affected by this—she became heartbroken that her father made her feel left out. Sometimes she would come to me with her concern. "Mom, Auntie Martha is my auntie, so why is my dad seeing her?" I was devastated and frustrated because my child was hurt and confused. I did not want my child to experience such anguish.

One day when her dad came by the apartment to see her, I confronted him. "What are you doing?" I asked. "What kind of signal are you sending to Latisha?"

"Are you jealous?" he replied in a smug manner.

I wanted him to be a man, to be responsible for the message he was sending to our daughter. It pained me even more to see that he did not care much for Martha—he did not want to live with her and take care of her children. He used my sister to get back at me, but the worst part is that it was at the expense of his own daughter.

Our argument grew to be very heated that day. He got angry and got loud, as usual, in an attempt to bully me into submission.

"It's none of your business what I do!" he declared.

"Stop, Daddy," Latisha cried, as Troy got louder and more boisterous. "Stop it!"

Allicia did not say anything. She crept into the closet and hid herself away, just as she used to do when she was a little child. She was not a stranger to his rage. She knew what he was capable of and, as usual, she was terrified.

He continued to shout, but I refused to give into his cowardly attempt at dominance over us I did not back down—whatever he said to me, I answered him with the same conviction. Finally, he stormed out and slammed the door behind him. For a moment, I stared at it and then I shook my head. When would he and I ever be able to have a decent discussion about our daughter without fighting?

While I was struggling with the demands of school, work and family, I had another issue to deal with—my sister Suzette spiraled into depression. She was pregnant and was contemplating an abortion. I was against it and talk her out of it, but, as a result, I ended up having to spend hours each day on the telephone with her. My studies had to be pushed onto the backburner while I focused on being an emotional support for her. Suzette gave birth in Montreal after being pregnant for only seven months. She was under so must distress that she left the baby in hospital. The baby was in turn sent to foster care. I took the matter to court and got legal custody of the baby. I was not living in Montreal; as a result, it was difficult to leave with the new born because his mother lived in Montreal. Therefore I advocated for Suzette's father to care for the baby—it was better for the baby because most of his relatives were in Montreal. After a week of court and social workers proceeding, I returned home to Toronto.

In Toronto, my studies continued to suffer—I was under so much pressure, I often became very emotional at the simplest conversation with my teachers. I ended up failing my last semester at Centennial College.

I reapplied to take over my last semester courses that I had failed. In the meantime, I landed a placement at the Toronto East Detention Centre. Following that placement experiences, I completed an additional placement at the Yorkly Youth Detention Centre, where I continued working on a part-time basis after completing the program.

On one occasion while working at the Youth Detention Centre, youth workers were doing their daily rounds, transporting troubled youths to different locations. I was at my post working when the scheduled transport van arrived with troubled youth. The other workers proceeded to escort the youth out of the van, but there was one girl who refused to budge.

"No way am I coming out," she protested.

I remained at my post observing the whole situation. Members of staff, managers and others were going back and forth trying to get her to vacate the vehicle, but to no avail. The girl would not come out. Finally, the decision was made to take her back to her former detention home. At this point I stepped in: "May I help?" I asked.

I got into the van and sat beside her. "Hi," I said, trying to make her comfortable in my presence. "How are you?"

"Fine," she replied in a sullen voice.

"What's your name?" I asked, wanting to put her at ease.

She answered briefly, giving her name

"Tell me something," I said. "I noticed all the other staff has attempted to help escort you out the van, but yet your still here. Why don't you want to leave? What's wrong?"

She briefly scowled as she looked out the window, "I am not going in there. There are only white people in there and I am not going in there with them."

"What am I?" I asked her. "Do I look white to you?"

"No."

"Listen to me. There are black girls in there and white girls in there, so you're not the only black person here. Come on inside and stop this silly behaviour."

"Really? There's a black person in there?" She looked surprised.

"Yes, there is. Now, come on."

She got up, came out with me—everybody's jaw dropped as I escorted her inside.

Later the supervisor called me into the office. "What did you say to that girl to get her out of the van when we could not get her out?" he asked.

"I told her she was not the only black person around here, and that she should stop being silly. With that, she came out."

"Really? That's all you said?" He was dumbfounded by my simplistic approach. "Thank you, Myrtle. You did a good job." That day I felt proud that I could make a difference. During my time of working there, black youths would have felt more at ease if there were more people of colour. It was a great experience in my life, the staff and I worked well together, and it was a memorable experience.

Seeing that most of my recent jobs were only on a part-time basis, I decided to take a course to become a call centre operator. I thought that maybe this would give me an opportunity to get a full-time position with an established company. During the Christmas holidays, there were no classes, so I was able to spend a little more time with the children. However, in the New Year my mother came from Montreal to spend some time with me. At the time my sister Suzette's children were also in my care—being responsible for them, my own children, as well as Mother, cast a heavy burden on me. I did not have a full-time job and with so many depending on me to fulfill their needs made it very stressful.

While staying at my home, my mother complained about excruciating pain in her neck—I could tell by just looking at her that she was suffering tremendously.

"Okay, Mother," I said firmly, "I'm taking you to the hospital."

She did not want to go, but I insisted. I took her to the bathroom, washed her and dressed her—she was in too much pain to help herself. Then I drove her to the hospital and alerted the emergency staff immediately of her pain. Fifteen minutes passed and no one attended to us. "If anything happens to my mother, I am holding you all responsible," I declared. I was not prepared to have her sitting there, suffering in a hospital waiting room. Shortly after, a nurse came over and checked my mother—she called the doctor immediately and the doctor later informed us my mother was having a mild heart attack. Mother was admitted into the hospital right away. The challenging part was to get her to eat the hospital food. She would only eat food I prepared and brought from home. This was time consuming for me, as I juggled duties as a parent, work, school and my ailing mother all on my own.

It was all getting to be too much for me, so I had to be stern with her. "Mother, you have to eat or you will die," I told her. I shocked her into submission, but I had to because she was all skin and bones.

Two weeks after the procedure, Mother was discharged from the hospital. I took her straight to the drug store at the mall to fill her prescription. When we got there, I realized that I had left the prescription at the hospital. I left her at the mall with the children and rushed back to the hospital to get it. By the time I returned, Mother had already smoked two cigarettes. "Mother, you spent all this time in the hospital. The doctor said you are not to smoke and here you are smoking. You are wasting my time," I said. "If you want to die, take yourself and go back to Montreal, but don't stay around me and do what you're not supposed to do."

It was a slap in the face after all I did for her and I refused to cater to her like an idiot. On top of that, she had the nerve to be angry at my children for telling me what she'd been doing behind my back. She became cold towards them, which made them very uncomfortable. It made me angry to think about how much I was sacrificing for my mother and yet she did not seem to care—not even for herself.

The money I used to purchase the heart medication for Mother came from my student loan. The money I was making at work went to paying all the bills and babysitting, so I did not have much money left over for other things. The expenses and all my responsibilities caught up with me—I failed all my exams for the January period. It was hard on me, taking care of everyone and I simply could not focus.

One of my teachers noticed there was something wrong, because I usually have good grades. She confronted me and I explained to her what I was going through at home; luckily she was willing to help me.

She made arrangements for me to take extra lessons so that I could get caught up. I was able to pass my exams and I soon got a placement with St. John's ambulance working in the call centre. This was a paid placement, but it was not nearly enough to cover all my financial needs.

At this point, I paid Mother's way back to Montreal and my sister's children returned to her. Their departure began to ease the pressure, but when I thought I was in the clear, Mother called me. "I don't have any food," she said. "I don't have a TV—I am staring at the walls." Money was still tight, but I wanted to do whatever I could to make my mother comfortable. I went to my friend's store and got a nineteen-inch television on credit. I got my cousin and a friend to drive with me to Montreal to deliver the television and some groceries to my mother. I didn't tell her I was coming because I wanted it to be a surprise.

I arrived early in the morning with the television and four full bags of groceries. She did not greet me or show any appreciation. All she said was: "Did you think I was lying? Is that why you've come?"

Instead of greeting me with joy, instead of showing appreciation for the effort I'd made in getting what she wanted and delivering it to her all the way in Montreal, this was the thanks I got.

My heart sank. I ignored her ungrateful remark—I did not have time or energy to argue with her. I took a short nap and then headed back home to go to work the next day. My mother could not find it within her to make me feel appreciated. Her reaction to my gifts was sarcasm, and it hurt. I left my mother's home that morning deep in thought. My situation was grim, as I was drowning in a sea of debt and there seemed to be no way of escape for me. I just was not earning enough even though I was working so hard. Did it make sense to be killing myself, working, when I was just sinking deeper and deeper in the mire? It was during this journey that a thought came to me—what if I was to go back to the States and leave my children with my cousin? I knew she would take care of them for me for a while. I thought maybe that would allow me to go away and seek a better living. I desperately needed to make a change for the better and I needed to do it quickly.

As soon as I returned to Toronto I acted on my plan. I assessed my financial situation. I had a month's rent put aside but I did not see how I would pay for the following month. I immediately went to the management rental office of the apartment building and spoke to the manager.

"I'm a single mom with three kids," I said. I don't have a full time job and I'm going to school. Instead of staying here not being able to pay rent I would like to live out my last month's rent and then I will leave. The manager understood my situation and agreed as to what I was asking for.

I waited for the kids to finish school and go on summer break. The same day school ended, I asked a friend to drive us to New Jersey to my Cousin Eva's place. I then left the girls and returned to Canada with my son that same night. I started packing my things for a storage unit. I also informed my school of my plans of not returning to complete the fall term. Two weeks later Tevin and I went back to the States to join Allicia and Latisha.

Aunt Bernice visited us in New Jersey from time to time, where she got to know the children. She always commented on how respectful and beautiful they were. While staying with my Cousin Eva, the children were registered to start school in late August. During the summer holiday they attend summer camp in Lake Wood. I tried my best to make sure my children had everything they needed. However, trying to survive, doing odd jobs like taking care of the elderly, was something I thought I could do back in Canada—life was still a struggle. Then, one day I received a call from Troy saying "if you don't take my daughter back to Canada I am going to call the police and tell them you took her" After three months of staying with my cousin I decided to return to Canada. The children and I stayed in Oshawa which was a suburb, east of the city from Toronto. We stayed for the next few months with Auntie Olivia.

Life in Canada did not prove to be much easier—suburban living created a new set of challenges. I wanted to keep my children in the same school they attended. I believe that keeping them in the same environment was beneficial to them because they were progressing well and I did not want to disrupt their learning process. I had to take the children to school every day and the commute from Oshawa to Scarborough was very draggy, especially on the highway during rush hour. Once they were in school I would start searching for jobs. I went to unemployment centers, I searched though newspapers and online at the library. Sometimes when I was not job hunting because I did not have the money for gas, I would linger around the children's school waiting for them to finish. When school was finished the children and I would travel back to Aunty Olivia. This was the weekly routine for my children and I and it was the only logical one because I did not see any other way of keeping the children in their school.

In the end I decided that staying in Oshawa was just too difficult. We left Aunt Olivia and stayed at the house of a friend who was living closer to the school. That helped a bit but still, we needed our own place.

My friend Prudence witnessed the struggles I was experiencing and said, "Let me talk to Terrence, I will see if he can rent you his basement apartment."

Prudence arranged things with her ex-husband and we had moved into his basement apartment. I acquired some of my furniture from storage and we set up our home within his basement. Eventually I was offered a position at St. Vincent de Paul, working with the mentally challenged. The money was not much, not enough to cover the cost of the apartment, and living expenses. Thankfully, the Social Service Department decided to provide me with the difference.

I spoke with Prudence in regards to getting a job at her workplace and she promised to let me know when they would be hiring. She was true to her word. She called me and said that they were hiring so I handed in my resume. Soon after I was called for an interview and on August of 2001, I was hired as a Personal Support Worker. It was difficult for me to hold on to both jobs because of the scheduling issue, so I made a decision to resign from St Vincent DePaul.

I was excited about my job at Kennedy Lodge. I knew it would be a challenge for me but I was finally doing the work I wanted to do after my grandmother's death. My job there was fulfilling, assisting the patients with what they could not do for themselves, gave me a great sense of satisfaction.

## XV

One day in April of 2002, while I was at work, I got a call from one of my cousins from New Jersey with some devastating news—Aunt Bernice was in the hospital. Upon hearing the news, I called her right away. At this point in time, we spoke frequently and were able to salvage our relationship. I loved Aunt Bernice and was just happy to rekindle a once damaged connection. I called many times and spoke with her while in the hospital and promised that I would take the children down to visit her during the summer holidays. Sadly, this did not happen. I got another call from the States, and this time it was to inform me that Aunt Bernice had passed away.

My mind raced back to our argument and how hurt I'd felt that she could even think that I would steal her money. My consolation was that the letter had been returned to her, thus proving my innocence. I also respected the fact that she had been honest enough and brave enough to call me and admit that she was wrong. I decided I would go to the funeral—I had to pay my last respects.

A few days before I left for the States I spoke with my cousin, Michelle, whom asked if I was attending the funeral.

"Is your mother coming?" she also asked.

"No, she's not coming," I replied. "A friend of mine is going to drive with me."

"Won't it look bad that you're taking your friend instead of your mother? Remember, its Aunt Imo's sister who died."

I thought about it for a moment. "Ok, I'll take her."

I called my mother to inform her of the day I was leaving to go to the States and asked if she would like to go with me to the funeral—she agreed to come. The trip involved my mother and I, with my three children—Allicia who was fifteen at the time, Latisha who was twelve and eight-year-old Tevin.

The journey down was fun. I remember each time I would try to pass McDonalds the children would scream out "Mom McDonalds is coming up don't pass it this time." We stopped along the way to eat and refresh ourselves. There were times, though, when the children got restless. I guess they were feeling cramped in a two-door sports car. They started bickering. "I don't want to be squished back here," one of them would say. "I want space," the other would complain. Allicia began doing things to annoy her little brother, including digging him in the ribs with her elbow.

It was hard dealing with that on a journey of several hours, so I ended up having to put Latisha in the middle to separate Allicia from her brother. Later, on one of our pit stops, I got a toy for Tevin—something to keep him occupied as we travelled.

In between spats, the children and their grandmother chatted amiably. They engaged in comfortable conversation, and the laughter was easy and frequent, something I can't remember ever doing with my mother. I was pleased that my children and my mother seemed to be getting along so well together.

When we finally arrived in New Jersey, I dropped Mother off at Uncle Lorenzo's house and then the children and I went to stay with my cousin Evelyn's. That night we saw Aunt Icema and Uncle Beb, who arrived from Jamaica for the funeral. Uncle Beb had met Allicia and Latisha, now he was being introduced to Tevin for the first time. He hugged and kissed them and said how happy he was to see them all. Still, even though there was a smile on his face, we could see the sadness hiding behind his eyes.

The day of the funeral was sad. As I drove in the church parking lot I notice the Hurst was already at the church, with a few family members in the Limousine. Not knowing what my experience would be as I approach the church, I was suddenly overwhelmed with emotions. As I slowly walked towards the coffin I became nervous and the tears began to fall. When I saw Aunty in the coffin, I notice she had lost a lot of weight. Her face looked a lot smaller but she was beautiful in her white dress. As I looked around in the church I could see lots of family members, the other person that melted my heart was my uncle Beb. He cried so much he could not sit still in the church. He kept pacing and crying and holding his hands up in the air. He kept shaking his head and crying—I think her death devistated him most of all.

On the other side of the church, my mother sat crying, but the sight of her tears did not faze me the way that Uncle Beb's tears pierced my heart. I had little empathy left for my mother; she took it from me long before Aunt Bernice's death. Mother often treated her sister with little dignity, leaving her alone in an empty apartment when she visited her in Montreal. I knew they did not get along too well and her tears only added to my resentment. To me, her tears were not ones of real sorrow—I don't think my mother was ever capable of that emotion.

I moved from my seat and went over to Uncle Beb. I hugged him and sat him down in the pew. I consoled him as best as I could. Eventually, he calmed down a bit before service started. It was a very emotional day. Uncle Lorenzo, Aunties' eldest brother, also really mourned her death. Later my aunt was laid to rest, once the funeral had ended, all the family members and guests went to a hall for the reception. By the time we returned to my cousin's house we were all exhausted so we went to bed.

When we were ready to leave New Jersey we had a lot of stuff because I had shopped for myself and my three children. Mother had shopped as well, plus she had a lot of Aunt Bernice's belongings that she planned to take back to Canada. We had a packed car when we were ready to return to Toronto.

We'd planned to get up very early that Monday morning, at around 4 a.m., to start our journey back to Canada. However, we did not head out until about 6 a.m. Tevin was supposed to have stayed behind with Aunt Icema because he did not have school. It would have been a great opportunity for the rest of the family to get to know him, but I gave into his wishes and decided to take him back with us.

By the time we got to Pennsylvania it was night time. I drove into a rest stop in Scranton and took out some money from the bank machine. I then sat in the car while mother went outside to smoke and the children played and burned off some energy. About forty-five minutes later we continued on our journey, driving along Route 81 North on the highway back to Canada. Sometime along this way, I decided to pull over so that Mother could take the wheel. I slowly hugged the breaks, getting ready to pull over. But I never got the chance—all of a sudden, I felt something slam into the rear end of the car. That's all I remember of that moment. Everything went black.

I was knocked unconscious for I don't know how long, I slowly opened my eyes and looked around. "What happened?" I tried to say, but nothing came out except a groan. Then, suddenly I remembered—we'd been hit from behind. I jerked upright and a sharp pain ripped through my body. I moaned out loud, clutching my chest. I looked around, anxious to see if my family was safe. I saw Mother in the passenger seat with her head back and her denture resting on her lip. Latisha was in the back with her head resting against the window with her eyes closed. I turned as far as I could and saw Allicia behind my seat, not moving—she was unconscious. I thought I heard Tevin whisper, "Mom, did we crash?"

My heart jerked inside me when I heard his faint voice. "My God, what has happened to us?" I thought.

I pushed at the door, trying to open it, desperate to get out. It was stuck fast. All I could do was wind the window down. I was trapped in the car, unable to sit up straight or breathe properly. I did not know what to do.

I gathered all my strength and I pulled myself up and out of the car, inch by inch through the window. The pain was shooting across my chest, spreading through my entire body, but I did not stop. I had to get out; I had to wake them up. Finally, I fell to the ground then scrambled up and around the front. I rushed around the front of the car to the door on my mother's side and pulled on the door. It did not budge. I pulled on the door handle as hard as I could. Nothing.

With a sob, I tried again but the door was jammed shut. Suddenly, I heard Latisha's voice: "Mom, my leg hurts."

I felt like a knife had been plunged into my heart. My child was hurt—her leg might even be broken—and I could not get to her. I peered in through the window and saw Allicia. She just lay there, not moving, not making a sound. "*Oh, dear God*," I thought, "*what am I going to do?*"

I ran back to the driver's side and leaned in as far as I could to grab little Tevin, who was sitting between his sisters. I reached over until I caught hold of him. He pushed his body forward and I kept on pulling until he was free at last, out through the driver's side window and onto the grass beside me. I peered in through the window again—all the others were there still stuck inside. How was I going to get to them? How could I pull them out? Tevin was small, but how in the world was I going to manage the others?

I walked back around the car and looked up. The car was down in a ditch, engine still running and light shining up into the night sky.

"Help!" I screamed. "Help!"

Excruciating discomfort were tearing across my chest, but the adrenilain rushing through my veins kept me from fainting as I scrambled up the ditch and onto the side of the road, screaming for help. None of the cars stopped and no one pulled over to help.

I kept on yelling until finally, when I looked up ahead, I saw a man on the top of the road on his cell phone. To my great relief, I saw another man coming down towards the car. "I smell gas," he said, and scurried over to turn off the engine.

Soon after, I heard the sirens approaching. The emergency crews jumped out of their vehicles and ran toward us. I told them what had happened. They wanted Tevin and me to move farther away so I grabbed some blankets from the car and they spread them out on the ground some distance away. They told us to lie down—they wanted to be able to work freely without us in the way.

There were ambulances for each of us, but little Tevin was scared to go alone. They let him ride in the same ambulance with me and rushed us away from the scene to the nearest hospital. Latisha was transported to a different hospital. Later I learned that they could not get Allicia and my mother out of the car. The back of the car had been pushed right up to the front—they had to cut off the top and lift them out. When they got Allicia out, her blood pressure was dangerously low, with the top reading being only twenty-nine. She had to be put on life support right there on the grass, next to the wreckage. Allicia was dying.

They got Mother and Allicia to the hospital even before we arrived. I found out they were airlifted to the hospital. As soon as I was wheeled in, a doctor rushed up to me. "Your mother is dying," he said. "Sign this." He thrusted a paper under my nose; all I could do was stare up at him in shock. He must have seen my distress because his face softened. "We were waiting on you to do the paperwork so we could operate," he said. "Please, sign here." A couple of hours later the doctor came and sat beside me. "How is my daughter?" I asked, searching his face, wanting an answer, but fearing his response. He looked at me and when he spoke his voice was quiet and serious.

"Your daughter is in a coma. She's had a haematoma," He revealed. "Her brain is filled with a lot of fluid and it's bleeding. We're just watching her—there is nothing we can do right now."

I froze, unable to speak, unable to lift the leaden weight that had fallen on my heart.

"She also has a broken hip," he continued.

I shook my head, trying to understand. It took a moment before I was able to hear the rest of what he was saying. Allicia's major injuries were a shattered hip and trauma to the brain, he told me.

For a while I was unable to speak. I swallowed. "How is my mother?" I whispered.

The seatbelt had squashed her so hard that it ruptured her spleen and she'd started bleeding profusely inside. They had to cut her open from top to bottom and wash her out. The spleen could not be saved so it had to be removed. He explained that the spleen is what fights infections, so they had to give her several injections to help her fight off infections, but she would still have to be cautious from now on. At this point my mother was also in a coma.

The doctor said that Tevin was shaken up, but he was fine. They couldn't give me much on Latisha, but they assured me that she was at a hospital, where patients go when they have non-life-threatening injuries—the hospital we were at specialized in treating trauma. I was still scared for Latisha, but I clung to any positive news they could give me—I had to, I had no other choice. I convinced myself that she would be fine.

"And you, Miss Morrison" he said, turning to me, "you have six cracked ribs and a fractured vertebra." He also mentioned. I had some gouges on the leg, but the fractured bones were the more serious of my injuries.

It was at that point that I finally found a moment to pause and think on the situation. I asked someone to call Latisha's father, Troy in Canada to let him know what had happened, then I got some calls through to our family back in New Jersey.

Next morning as I sat up in bed waiting to be release, I looked up and there was Latisha's father walking towards me with Latisha by his side. I was filled with relief and joy—my second daughter was all right. It was not until I saw Latisha that I learned that the glass from the back had gouged a bit of the flesh under her chin and she'd gotten splinters in her hand. Despite this, she would be alright and I thanked God for that.

When Troy was leaving to head back to Canada, he took both Latisha and Tevin with him. Then, out of nowhere, like an angel my stepsister appeared—she was one of the last persons I expected to see.

"Oh my God!" I exclaimed. "What are you doing here?"

"Martha told me what happened," Crystal said. "I came here as soon as I heard."

I learned that Crystal was now living in Pennsylvania, about an hour away from the Scranton Hospital. I'd felt all alone so far from home, away from friends and family. But now, knowing that Crystal was there, I felt relieved. I knew she would be there when we needed her.

I was released from the hospital that same day. I only had cracked bones, so the doctors advised me to take some pain medication and let the injuries heal on their own. From there, I went to stay at the Ronald McDonald house, where persons from out of town with relatives in the hospital were allowed to stay at no cost. Both accommodation and meals were provided for free. It was a nice, clean place to stay—I appreciated that. I remained there so I could be near my child and my mother.

At this point, I did not have any clothing to my name. The emergency people had cut through my clothing to attend to my injuries—I had gone to the Ronald McDonald House in nothing but my hospital gown. Crystal was nice enough to bring me some clothes.

Days passed and Allicia remained in a coma. Her body flexed from time to time. Initially I was elated to see her twitch in the hospital bed, hoping it was a sign she would wake up, but the doctor said she was unconscious and the movements were involuntary. They had to strap weights on her legs, so she would not aggravate her broken hip. I visited her daily—I wanted to be the first one there once she opened her eyes.

A couple of days later my brothers Abraham and John and my sister, Martha, came from Canada to see us. We also had family visiting us from New Jersey—those who had been at Aunt Bernice's funeral. Uncle Beb came as well but he had to rush to emergency ward, as the stress of seeing what happened to us was causing him heart problems. He was released later that day and so he was able to return to New Jersey.

Allicia lay in the coma day after day. For more than a week, there were no significant changes. Her dad and her aunts came to visit her from Florida and the Bronx, but still, Allicia lay in the coma. After another week her leg began to twitch uncontrollably and doctors were concerned that it was healing in this crooked form. The situation remained grave. The doctors needed to operate as soon as possible but they could not—not until she woke out of the coma.

Each day that I talked to Latisha and Tevin on the phone they would say, "Mom, you're not doing it right."

"You have to talk to Allicia, Mom," Latisha said. "You can't stop. You have to keep talking and talking and talking. Then she'll wake up."

"Latisha," I said, "I talk to Allicia until my mouth is dry. When I'm finish talking, I'm just so tired."

"You know what, Mom? I'm going to show you," Latisha said. "I'm going to come and wake Allicia up—you'll see."

Troy agreed to bring the kids back. He made the journey to the border, but there he ran into problems. The immigration officers wanted to make sure he was not kidnapping the children, removing them from Canada without the knowledge of their mother. In order to verify his story, they took Tevin into a room all by himself and questioned him. When he told them that his mother had been in a serious collision and in the hospital and they were all on the way to visit her, they finally accepted the story and let them enter the USA.

When they arrived at the hospital, Latisha pulled some CDs out of her bag. I was surprised and happy to see she brought Allicia's favorite music. She put the music on—it was '*Meditate*', the gospel song by Out of Eden, filled the room. The music played for just a few minutes when Latisha's father walked over to the bed.

"Allicia, wake up." His voice was strong, booming. It was a command, not a plea. "Wake up, Allicia."

To my astonishment, Allicia blinked. For the past two weeks, I had been sitting by my daughter's side, begging her that if she could hear my voice she should just squeeze my hand. Do something, I would beg, anything—just let me know that you are here. But there was nothing. Now, for the first time, there was a sign of recognition, some kind of acknowledgement that she was aware in some way of what was going on around her.

"Allicia, wake up. You have to wake up now." Latisha's voice was high pitched and clear which pierced through the fog that surrounded her older sister.

Allicia blinked again and then she turned her head. I felt my heart jerk inside my chest. I moved closer to the bed. My daughter was coming back to me.

"Say hi to Shelly, your baby sister," Troy said in the same authoritative voice. He was speaking as through she was awake and defiant, not to someone whose body had gone through so much trauma and locked away in a coma. There was no gentleness, no hesitation in his speech.

"Say hi to her," he demanded.

I watched, not breathing, as my daughter continued to blink. And then she opened her eyes. My jaw dropped as I stared at her, tears filled my eyes, my heart felt as though it would burst out of my chest.

Over the years, Allicia had always been fearful of Troy. She respected his authority and was quick to obey him. Today, her fear of disobeying him seemed to be the key that unlocked her sleeping brain.

Allicia looked at us, from one to the other, and then slowly she raised her hand. She was reaching for the baby, the toddler in Troy's arms. She'd remembered his daughter, the little sister she loved to play with and cuddle.

For a moment I stared at my daughter and the tears were on the verge of spilling over onto my cheeks. "Thank you, God," was all I could whisper. She had lost so much weight that it made her eyes look big in that little face, but it was the most beautiful sight I had seen since the accident.

I hurried out of the room to get the doctor. Within minutes, a team of a doctors and nurses were in Allicia's room, examining her. They did not want Allicia out of the coma totally because they had been waiting all this time for her to come out of her unconscious state so that they could perform surgery on her hip. Meanwhile, Mother was still in the hospital recuperating. I was getting ready to go with my daughter to another hospital, but I did not want to leave my mother alone. So, I spoke to the doctor about having her released and sent back to Canada. I called my brother Abraham to come and take our mother home.

Allicia was immediately moved from Scranton Hospital, where she had been since the accident, to Hershey Hospital. The surgery would be performed there a couple of days later. The doctor at Hershey Hospital sat me down and explained the risks of the surgery. He expressed to me that my daughter might not come out of the surgery alive—I felt a rush of panic flood my body when he said that to me. My daughter has just survived the coma, only for me to lose her in surgery?

I knew what the doctor was doing—he was preparing me for death. If she did not make it, I would already have been told to expect this. If she lived, I would be thankful. At this point, I felt like telling the doctor that I did not want Allicia to undergo surgery. I was so afraid of losing her, but I had no other options. If she were to ever walk again she had to have the operation.

The night before Allicia's surgery, I did not sleep at all. My thoughts were on my daughter the whole night. On top of that, I was in excruciating pain from my cracked ribs. It was so bad that the slight tensing required to unscrew the cap on my medicine bottle was more than I could bear. Luckily, my brother John was there with me. Troy took the children back to Canada, so John was my only company at this hospital. It was he who had to open the bottle of medication so that I could get something to relieve the pain.

Tuesday dawned and, as I stared out at the sunrise, I breathed deeply, trying to prepare myself mentally. It was the day of Allicia's surgery and I was exhausted from the lack of sleep and weak from the constant pain. When I got to the hospital later that morning, Allicia was wheeled into the operating room and then my real agony began. I was imagining my first baby lying there on the table, needles piercing her skin, scalpels cutting away at her flesh—they might even have saws cutting through her bones. I could not bear to think about it.

And my own pain, despite the medication, was getting worse. Allicia's doctor came into the lounge to explain the operation he would soon be performing on her. He looked at my face and he must have seen my suffering. He referred me to one of his colleagues for my pain. This new doctor made a request for my file to be sent to him from the Scranton Hospital. Within a few minutes he had received it. He went through it quickly then looked at me.

"You tell me, Miss Morrison. What can I do for you?" His voice was calm and soothing.

Despite my intense pain, I spoke in a steady voice. "I would love for you to take this pain away." It was a genuine plea for relief.

The doctor nodded then wrote a prescription for thirty pills, but he warned that this medication was very strong and could be addictive—I had to be careful. When I arrived at the pharmacy they expressed the same warning the doctor had advised earlier. Instead of accepting the thirty pills written on the prescription I asked the pharmacist to only give me ten. I knew I was not going to get addicted because I don't usually like to swallow pills unless I am in unbearable pain. For now, I just needed some relief so I could think clearly on the day Allicia needed me most.

The painkillers the doctor prescribed must have been one of the strongest, if not the best, in the United States. When I took the first pill I felt like I'd been set free. I felt no pain, not even a twinge—absolutely nothing. With this new found relief, I went back to the waiting lounge and was able to sit quietly and focus my thoughts on my daughter's surgery.

After hours of waiting the head surgeon, Doctor Reid finally walked into the waiting room to see me. I stared at him, not able to breathe, but when I saw the smile on his face I exhaled in utter relief.

"The surgery went well," he said. "We had to give her blood, but she's recovering well."

"Thank you, doctor," I whispered. I was so overwhelmed I did not know what else to say to him.

I went straight to the ward where I had been told Allicia was recovering. Allicia laid there in the bed, still unconscious, but she was alive and for that moment, it was enough to fill me with gratitude. Hours later, when she finally awoke Allicia, stared up at me with huge eyes. She seemed to have lost even more weight since the surgery, but that was something that I could fix with good food and care.

When the doctors visited Allicia on Thursday, two days after the surgery, they were stunned at her quick recovery. She had recovered so well that the doctors said she had advanced seven days ahead.

As she began to recover, Allicia's first memory was of her beloved pet, Ashley. "How is Ashley?" she whispered, her thin face glowing with the pleasant memories. The black Labrador-Retriever had come into our family when it was only five weeks old and immediately bonded with us. Allicia loved Ashley from the first day she held her, in her arms. The puppy grew into a lively and loving dog that would run to the door to greet the children as soon as they got home from school.

Ashley became so protective of the family that no one could hug any of us when she was around. If anyone thought of raising a hand to us, they could not do so in her presence. Since she'd come into our lives, she'd been our personal guardian angel, and an important part of our family.

Although the recollection of family members took a while longer for Allicia, the memory of Ashley remained at the forefront in her mind, despite her recent trauma.

The doctors scheduled Allicia for a series of mental assessments and that was when I got news that burst my bubble of elation. I was told that Allicia's brain had reverted to that of a five—or six-year-old. The worry crept into my mind as I thought about what this would mean. Would she recover fully? Would I ever get my fifteen-year-old daughter back? Allicia had to be taught how to put on her shoes and socks, count and spell simple words and how to brush her teeth. They even had to teach her how to eat because she was just gobbling up her food with her hand, pushing it into her mouth as if she did not remember how to use her utensils properly. When she was eating someone had to watch her because we were afraid she would choke.

On July 29, thirteen days after Allicia's surgery, she was transferred from Hershey Hospital in the States to Bloor view Macmillan Hospital in Toronto via a small airplane. When we arrived at Pearson International Airport in Toronto, the ambulance personnel was waiting for us and immediately took us to Bloorview. When we arrived we were restricted to the hospital room—quarantined until they could assess us to ensure that we hadn't brought any germs with us from the hospital in the USA. At first it was very disturbing to be a hazard, but I later realized that it was for the safety of all the patients at the hospital.

Allicia spent three months at Bloor View Macmillan Hospital, where she was given physical therapy every day. At first she had to use a wheel chair, and then she progressed to using a walker. Afterwards Allicia started using a crutch and finally after months of therapy she was able to use a cane. Throughout her stay, Allicia was well taken care of—she even attended school at the hospital so she would not fall behind. Luckily, all her expenses were covered by my car insurance and OHIP—even my lost wages were covered. They also provided someone to assist me with my housework as I was still recovering from the cracked ribs and fractured vertebra. Allicia also got a personal assistant to help with her daily activities.

Over time Allicia came around, eventually beginning to move about on her own. She now had a plate in her hip with four screws; she is adjusting to it little by little. By November, she was officially released from the hospital and was ready to go home. She went back to her regular high school and, with the help of educational assistants, she began her full-time studies. She continued to work with a case manager, a speech pathologist and a physiotherapist. She also had a personal helper to assist her around the house. As Allicia recovered she moved gingerly around the house, trying to get back to doing all the things a teenager would normally do.

However, in those days I had to watch her constantly to prevent accidents. I could not leave her alone in the kitchen, as she often placed things on the stove and then walk away, forgetting all about it. I realized that it would take some time for her brain to fully recover, so I was very patient with her.

Even with the help of the educational assistants, schoolwork became difficult for Allicia. Although she had done some studies at the school in the hospital, she had missed so much of the first semester she was told that she would not be able to graduate with the rest of her class. Allicia refused such fate. She left home every day with her walker and she navigated her way around school, going to all her classes, determined to finish with the rest of her class. With the help of a support team she began to work on her lessons and on her recovery.

There were many people who played important roles in Allicia's recovery. We were fortunate to have Kim as her case manager. Throughout the time that she worked with Allicia, Kim was efficient and caring, and a real problem solver. She ensured that my daughter had everything she needed to facilitate her recovery. Kim hired individuals that helped Allicia with her studies and helped around the house. After Kim was assigned elsewhere, Barb took over as Allicia's case manager. Both Allicia and I missed Kim, and it took us a little while to adjust to the new manager, but Barb proved herself to be quite proficient and we were soon impressed with her care.

Allicia was also assigned a speech/language pathologist. Patty worked alongside Allicia by doing various activities that helped build on her pronunciation and vocal skills. For example, Patty would interact with Allicia by talking; reading books aloud, using objects that helped to stimulate Allicia's language development. Patty also used repetitive exercises to help build Allicia's speech and language skills. After the accident Allicia spoke very fast and as a result, she stumbled over her words, making it difficult to understand her. Over time, and through Patty's patient instructions, Allicia finally began to speak normal again. Patty would visit Allicia both at home and at her school. Overall, Patty made sure that Allicia got all the attention that she needed for a full recovery.

Before the accident Allicia was a soft, gentle-spirited individual and quite an introvert, but after the accident she became more bold and assertive. She became a person who was determined to prove others wrong. The accident really pushed her to strive for success and no one was going to stand in her way.

I was relieved, in 2007 when she met Brandi, an education assistant who was closer to her age. They seemed to hit it off immediately, and I was glad when they settled down into a comfortable working relationship. Allicia worked with several other support staff and I appreciated their dedication in helping her recover from her trauma. As a result of her determination, and with the strong support team that was provided, Allicia was able to graduate right on schedule with the rest of her class. She did not let anything stop her from achieving her goal, not her absence while in hospital nor her challenges as a result of the accident.

On the night of her prom she was beautiful, dressed in a backless white gown with black ribbons all around the skirt. She wore flat shoes, since heels would only aggrevate her injuries. She and her handsome date were picked up by a Hummer limousine, which she and her closest friends had rented. The next day she prepared for the graduation ceremony. The entire graduating class wore white dresses, white robes and white hats to signify purity, the tradition at Notre Dame Catholic Girls' School. They all looked like angels that day.

My daughter had come a long way from the accident when someone had to reteach her the ABC's and 123's. Now she was a high school graduate; a fighter who had achieved her goal and I could not have been more proud.

## XVI

By this time, while Allicia was recovering, Mother came to stay with us. Although I was back at work, I was only handling light duties. The insurance company ensured I would not have to do any work that was too strenuous during my recuperation. I was still going through physical therapy, getting regular massages to ease the tight muscle pain.

I worked the night shift, and in the mornings, when I got home from work; Mother would ask me to take her to John's apartment to spend the day babysitting. I agreed because I need that time to sleep. This went on for a while she was worn out from going back and forth to John's home. The responsibility that was placed on her while she was there was a bit intense. One day, I saw how exhausted she looked, I asked her to take it easy; to have her breakfast and take her time before she rushed over to John place. "John needs a baby sitter," she retorted. "Laura is gone to work and John needs to rest. When I am there he can rest."

"Mother, John is a big man," I said. "John moved on, got married and had kids, so let him take care of them. You don't have to keep pushing yourself like this. Stay home a while longer and take your time and eat. After you eat, you can go."

"No," she insisted, shaking her head.

One morning I returned home tired from doing the night shift and was in no mood to take mother to my brother's home so I went to bed. I was asleep when someone woke me up. It was Allicia.

"Mom, Grandma is gone."

I sat up, confused. "Gone where?"

"Grandma said she doesn't know where she is going. She's just leaving."

That's what she'd told Allicia, but she could not fool me. I know she had a hidden agenda. She did not say a word to me about leaving. After I had opened my home to her, ensuring that she would have a room of her own, she just packed up and left. It must have something to do with the insurance money, I thought.

I figured that because Mother was expecting some money from the insurance company, she did not want to be in my care when it arrived. She probably did not want me to have anything to do with it. I guess she felt it was better if she stayed with John and then they would take care of the money when it came. For me, it did not matter either way—I had no desire for her money. I was just disappointed that she had not even had the courtesy to say goodbye; after I was trying so hard for us to have a relationship.

Once she'd moved out of my home, Mother began to say that I took her to the United States and tried to kill her. I did not dignify her declaration with an answer; that would have made it seem like there was some truth to what she was saying. I figured the best solution was to ignore her.

Still, the situation between Mother and I got worse and the tentative relationship we had formed was going downhill. She did do her own thing and again we drifted apart. Eventually, she realized that she and John's eldest daughter could not get along. In the end, I was the one she called to rescue her. I went to John's place to pick her up, and my own brother, looked at me and called me terrible names. John, who used to be my closest sibling, who lived in my home since he was fifteen or sixteen years old, a brother whom I took in my home over and over with his family, was now turning around and cursing me. I could not believe the level of disrespect.

It was then that I found out that John could be a very vindictive person—no matter what you did for him it was as if you never did enough. A big part of the problem was that he would not stand on his own two feet. Each apartment John moved into, he would get in trouble by not paying his rent and ended up moving back in with me. John and his family lived at my home for a year, maybe two, then move on again only to return soon after.

Still, I could not bring myself to vilify my brother's actions. He held a special place in my heart when he stayed with me at the Ronald McDonald House when Allicia was in the hospital. As soon as he heard me crying John would jump up from his cot and be by my side every time I called out for my daughter in the middle of the night.

John and his family ended up moving in with one of my friend. I am not sure why she did it, but she accommodated my mother, my brother, his wife and his kids. Mother moved from this home to an apartment, then another, until she moved into an apartment in Abraham's building. John eventually got his own place but, for my part, I tried not to get involved. My brother was a married man with a family and he needed to be left alone to get on with his life like a responsible man.

\* \* \*

I worked hard on being a good mother to my children, supporting them both emotionally and financially. However in 2004, things became more difficult for me—I needed help. I reached out to Curtis, Tevin's father, and told him "I need you to do your part and start supporting your son, if you don't—I will have to take you to court."

"You do what you have to do", he responded coldly. He probably thought I was bluffing, but like he said, I did what I had to do. I got all the necessary paper work completed, but when I went to serve him with the summons, he refused to take the papers from me. I was on my way to the police station when I saw a police car. I stopped them and asked for their advice.

"Tell him what is in it," they told me. "If he still does not take it, drop it at his feet and say you have been served."

I did exactly as I was told and then walked away. That was when Curtis realized that I was not joking. By that time it was too late. In the end he suffered because he refused to willingly work out an agreement with me. Once the situation was placed before the court, there was no turning back. I could have settled for a couple hundred dollars a month, instead, he had to abide by an amount set by the court, and the court was not as lenient as I would have been. I'm not sure if Curtis resented the fact that I took him to court to make him support his son. As far as I was concerned, I had given him the opportunity for us, as parents to work out a reasonable agreement. Through his own defiance, he ended up paying the price.

Since the time he was instructed to start paying child support, Curtis saw Tevin a few times, but he did not spend the time a boy needs with his father. I was very disappointed about that.

When Tevin got older, I sent him to the Bahamas to visit Curtis's mother. I wanted him to establish a relationship with his grandmother and the rest of his father's side of the family. Despite this, his relationship with his father never went anywhere. This is one thing I wish I could change for my son—I would love for him to have the love and attention from his father.

Following the accident it took a long time for me to recover, both physically and emotionally. One of my greatest challenges was being comfortable behind the steering wheel. Even in 2005, three years later, I did not want to sit in the drivers seat of a car while traveling on the highway, not even as a passenger. After a while, I decided to try, but each time I began to drive the memory of the accident would flash through my mind. My palms got damp and my hands trembled. I ended up pulling over by the side of the road, fearful that someone else was going to run into the back of my vehicle.

For a long time I only drove on local roads and avoided the highways altogether. I began to depend on friends and family members to drive me on the expressways. Eventually, I had to tackle them. I could not keep hiding forever.

After years of fearing the highway, I called the insurance company and informed them about this paralyzing fear. They were very understanding and made arrangements for me to work with a driving instructor who could boost my confidence. When I started the lessons, it was if I was learning to drive for the first time—I was a bundle of nerves. It was like my worst nightmare each time I approached a corner. Once, I came to a complete stop, unable to go any further. Even after several months of lessons, I approached each corner with fear.

"I'm trying my best to help you," my instructor said, "but I can only do so much. This does not seem to be working. I think you need some other type of help."

I was assigned a counsellor and after a few sessions, I went back to my driving instructor and began lessons again. He was patient and, although I could see that he had a stern personality, he was always gentle with me. For that, I was grateful.

"You don't have to hold the steering wheel so tight, Myrtle," he said quietly. "Just relax and drive. You can do it—I trust you."

I tried to take his advice, I did my best to stay calm, but nothing worked. Each time I approached a corner, I would slow down, nervous and trembling. Finally, I had a talk with my instructor.

"I appreciate all that you've done for me, and all you've taught me," I told him. "But I don't think that more lessons will help. I guess I will just have to continue practicing on my own. I will just have to be patient and I will wait for the time it takes for me to get over this fear."

I was true to my word and I kept driving on the highway, sometimes with friends and sometimes alone. Eventually, some confidence returned with years of practice.

## XVII

After creating a family of my own, I would sometimes wonder what my life would have been like if I'd had a father in my life. How different would things have been if I knew who my father really was? Where are my roots? These are questions that have haunted me over the years.

A few years after my first connection with the Morrison family, I heard that the eldest brother Tyrone—the same one who had reached out to me—had died. My connection with the family was now primarily through Dane. His son was working at the airport in Jamaica and I was happy to meet him there on one of my trips. He was so helpful to me that, when he asked for an invitation letter to come to Canada, I did not hesitate to provide one. He got the visa and came up to Canada for a visit.

To this day I love both families dearly. I still do not know who my real father is, but would have been happy to have a relationship with either one of the two gentlemen.

At one point I thought about having a DNA test done with Charles. I was burning to know who my real father was. I never approached him with the idea though; I just kept it to myself.

One day, I called my mother and told her my doctor needed to know my medical history, to know if cancer ran in my family. She refused to tell me who my father was—no matter what I said, she would not budge. Instead, she gave me a totally different story: she said that she'd been raped.

All she would say was that during the period that she was working in her sister's shop someone came into her room one night and raped her. What my mother was doing, in essence, was trying to shift attention away from my curiosity.

As I think back on my past, on my search for love from mother or father, I sometimes wonder what my life would have been like if my mother had behaved differently toward me. She always withheld her love from me—she even denied me the love of a father. I might as well have been an orphan.

At this point in my life, I don't know what role my mother would play—I gave up on creating some sort of a real mother-daughter connection. My demands of her were simple—I just wanted her to love me.

\* \* \*

One day in 2004 Terry picked up my mother. We were going to drop her off at John's home and, Terry saw that Mother and I needed to talk; he pulled into a nearby parking lot.

"Go ahead and talk," he said.

I turned to Mother and that's when the floodgates opened. "You really hurt me," I said. I talked about the incidents with her husband and how stressful it had been for me, trying to stay out of his way, and having her curse me even though I was the victim and he was the perpetrator. I went into detail as to how I suffered at the hands of my stepfather.

Mother stared at me, and then she turned to Terry: "I saw them with my own eyes, Terry," she said. "With my own eyes."

I sucked in my breath. "Mother, how could you lie like that?"

"You saw your daughter and your husband and you walked away and did nothing?" Terry's voice was hard. "Do you expect me to believe you? You would have hit the ceiling mother."

"Yes, Terry, yes," she insisted. "I saw it."

"Oh God, Mother, please." I shook my head. "How can you say these things?" Tears of frustration filled my eyes.

Finally, when Mother saw how much her words hurt me, she said, "It wasn't my fault—it was my husband." Her refusal to take any responsibility hurt me more than anything—as a mother I would do anything to protect my children.

This was my attempt in reaching out to my mother, a simple apology and "I love you" would have been sufficient, in fact, that is all I wanted from her. It deeply disturbed me that she showed no remorse at all. A stranger from outside would be likely to come into the house and get more love than I would get as her daughter.

When I lived with her in Montreal, her husband's cousins would sometimes visit and I use to watch her joking, playing and laughing with them. I, on the other hand, would be in the background just watching, like an outsider.

My stepfather never apologized either. It was hard when I used to visit them and take my children to their home. He used to cook for us and I had to bottle everything up inside and put on a pleasant face. For the sake of the children, I had to try to put it behind me. But his failure to acknowledge what he did wrong would never devastate me as much as my mother's perpetual denial. The countless sexual abuse I endured by family members made it difficult for me to trust men. How do I know who cares for me and who does not? It is a question I still grapple with to this day.

On the other hand, unlike my family, Terry has been such a source of support. Many times when I would go out of town, Terry is the one person I could trust with the care of my children. He's been a lifeline to us. There were times when I had no milk, no sugar and no food in the house—at those times I never had to explain anything to him.

"Don't bother to say anything," would be his response. "I'm on my way."

Just like that. He would come over, look around, and whatever was missing he would come back with it. Terry has done so much for us over the years. At the time when my cousin introduced him to me she already had a daughter with him but the relationship did not work, however, they remained as friends. Over the years he got married, so he was basically a big brother to me, one that I treasure.

"If you get to know Terry, he will be a good friend to you." Michelle could have never spoken truer words.

# XVIII

In February of 2006, I got news that Aunt Icema was sick and in the hospital in Jamaica. I was very upset—she was someone I could depend on. She'd made sure my siblings and I made it to Canada in one piece. She was always there for my children and me. Whenever I visited Jamaica, I always went to see her; she made sure our stay was always enjoyable. Now she was sick and could not take care of herself anymore.

It hurt me to hear this about my aunt. I knew I had to do something to make sure she was well taken care of. I went to Jamaica and made arrangements for Donna to take care of her. She was not financially able to assist Aunt Icema, but I took charge of her financial needs. It was a heavy burden on me at the time, but I felt I had to do this for her. Her brothers and sisters were helping out with whatever they could afford, but it was still not enough and I wanted all her needs to be met.

Aunt Winnie was in Jamaica visiting Aunt Icema when I got there. I was very happy to see both of my aunts. I could see that Aunt Icema was not doing well, but I made every effort to assist her in every way I could. I had long talks with her so she would not feel lonely and during the day, I lay beside her and kept her company.

Just before I had to go back home, the thought of leaving her, not sure that I would see her alive again, hit me hard. I had to keep reassuring myself she was going to be fine. I prayed, put everything in the Lord's hands, and asked Him to take care of her.

While in Jamaica, I visited Uncle Beb and the family in the country. We talked about Aunt Icema's illness. Uncle Beb himself was also not doing so well.

I returned to Canada feeling distraught. However, Aunt Icema and I continued to talk on the phone and, each month, I made it my duty to send money to Donna to cover her expenses.

Aunt called me one day, saying that she did not want to stay with Donna anymore. She wanted to go home to her husband. I asked Aunt to put Donna on the phone.

"Donna," I said, "Auntie wants to go home. Remember, whatever Auntie wants, Auntie gets."

I called my cousin Leron in the city and asked him to pick up Aunt Icema and take her to her home in the country. Her husband was very happy for her return. Most of the family members in the country would visit her from time to time and assisted in caring for her.

Aunt Icema was diagnosed with bone cancer. This seemed to be one of the worst forms of cancer. It was so bad that if she sneezed too hard, the bones in her jaw would crack. A few weeks later, I heard that Auntie had fallen off the bed and cracked a few ribs. I spoke with her on the phone two days later. It was the last time I spoke to her, as she passed away the very next day.

The news of Auntie's death still came as a shock, even though I knew she wasn't going to live much longer, but I still never expected it to happen so soon. I started making arrangements to go to Jamaica and to take the children with me. I knew this would be a sad experience for them, but especially for Tevin, as she had helped care for him as a baby. She had adored him, so I felt it was important for me to take him along.

On my arrival in Jamaica, I dived right into planning Aunt Icma's funeral. I took the bulk of the cost, but some family members pitched in what they could afford. I made sure that my aunt was laid to rest in a manner that made the family proud. Aunty had a beautiful casket, the funeral was taped, and the burial was very joyful, full of love and memories that would keep Aunty alive.

After putting my aunt to rest, I returned to Canada and focused on my family and my job at the nursing home. However, in October of that same year, a traumatic experience at the workplace destroyed my calm environment. It was about 7:15 a.m. and I was looking for a health care worker to ask if he was going to be part of the unit team. Each time I called the name of the staff member, I heard a groaning sound, as if someone was responding. Not knowing where the sound was coming from, I crept down the hallway. I saw a room and the door was closed. I pushed it open and peeked in. Across the room, at the closet door I saw a pale figure. I pondered if that was a picture or a person; from where I was standing I could not tell if it was a figure or a picture hanging on the door. I called a co-worker over. "Look over there," I said. "Is that a picture or someone hanging on the door?"

She gasped. "Myrtle, someone's hanging on the door."

"You're joking." I stared at her then back at the figure, realizing it was a corpse

I informed the nurse on the unit and then informed management "I think somebody hanged himself upstairs," I blurted out.

"What?" someone said? "Call 911."

"Come with me," one of the nurses said, taking charge. She made me take her to the location. We found the body still hanging there, a belt tight around the neck. The nurse examined him—the man had slit his wrists. The bloody pair of scissors was on the bed.

The nurses arrived to assess the body to see if he was still alive. Another resident was also staying in the room therefore; we had to remove him from the scene. A co-worker pulled the drape so that I did not have to look at the body, so that the resident could be escorted out the room.

It was then that I started to feel the panic rising inside me. I had seen death many times, as I had been working with the aged for over thirty years. I had never seen someone take their own life—nothing this gruesome. I had spoken with him just the day before; I served him his tea. He'd been such a jovial man. But when I think of him, his gentle smile does not enter my mind right away—his hanging body will forever haunt my memories.

The police arrived on the scene. They interviewed me and then I was told that I could go home. I was in such shock that the next day, I could not go to work. I could not find the courage to enter my workplace. It got so bad that I could not even drive on the street past the nursing home. All I kept seeing was the man hanging from the door.

I ended up having to work with a therapist for six months. Each time I drove by my workplace I had to cover my face with my hand. Later, I was able to drive past the grounds without averting my gaze. As part of my therapy, I then had to drive into the parking lot with a friend until I was able to do it by myself. For the next step, I had to enter the building. The administrator, Donna, was very understanding. She met me at the door and took me on a tour of the building as if she were reacquainting me with my surroundings.

"Myrtle, do you remember the dining room? Over here," she pointed, "this is where you used to seat the people. And that's where the elevator is, Myrtle. Don't forget."

As we walked along she kept on talking, reminding me of all the different areas in the building. She took me to the third floor, the same floor where I had found the body but I would not walk around, I stayed in one small area; I still needed time. One day Donna took things a step farther—she brought me to the room where I had seen the body hanging. Then she showed me the closet. My heart pounded as I approached it. She opened the closet.

"See, Myrtle, it's nice in here." She opened the door wider. "And there's the picture of Jesus. There's a lady staying in this room now." She kept chattering on, obviously trying to make me relax. "There's nothing to worry about."

Inside, my body had turned to jelly—everything inside me was shaking. Still, I tried to put on a brave face. When I finally left that room, my palms were damp and my legs were shaking, but as I followed Donna down the hallway, I took a deep breath and straightened my shoulders, determined that one day I would beat my fear.

Once, when I went downtown to one of my meetings with the therapist, I could not drive back. I felt nervous and was shaking all over. I had no idea what was going on. I called Terry to pick me up and drive me home. He came with my friend, Donna. She drove my car while he brought me home.

It took a long time before things went back to normal for me. Eventually, I learned to block out the image that would present itself to me each time I went on the third floor. Over time, I managed to suppress the memory so that I could do my job.

But then, as life often goes, it threw me another curve ball. While at work, I often went most of my day without eating. I remember one evening; I started feeling so dizzy that I asked a nurse to take my blood pressure. "Fifty over sixty," she said, frowning. "You're like a walking dead." She walked away and left me standing there.

I stared at her retreating back, shocked at her statement.

That evening I took my break as usual. I returned from dinner when I heard a call bell ringing. I went into the room to answer it. I assisted the resident and was leaving the room when the nurse in charge passed by—it was the same nurse who had read my blood pressure earlier.

"Why are you just coming back from break?" she demanded. "You know you're not supposed to overstay your break time."

"I did not just come back from my break," I said, puzzled at her aggressive attitude. "I was in the room checking on the resident."

She refused to believe me. Her face darkened in a scowl. Seeing that I would only lose if I tried arguing with her, I left things alone and went on with my duties for the rest of the shift.

The next day I returned to work and, around supper time, I started to have the same feeling again. I felt like the whole place was getting darker. I went to see the Assistant Director of Care.

"I'm not feeling well," I told her.

"Okay, Myrtle, go and sit over there," she said.

She called the nurse to check my blood pressure. I think this time it was about seventy over sixty.

"You'd better go home," the Director of Care said.

I called Terry to come and get me. I left with him soon after. I did not bother to call my doctor because I would not have been given an appointment to see her the same day. I knew I would be told to come in the following week so I did not bother.

In the meantime, things were becoming uncomfortable at work. I had a co-worker who was assigned to work upstairs. On this particular occasion, she and the nurse in charge wanted me to move to the floor to which she was assigned and then she would work on my floor. They'd always walked over me, but this time I wouldn't allow them to do so—I'd had enough of being pushed around. Because I refused to be bullied into moving, my co-worker got upset and began turning her back to me each time I worked with her. She refused to speak to me.

One day I was so fed up, I went to the nurse in charge. "This girl and I do not work well as a team," I said. "I can't deal with her attitude today. I would like to work with someone else."

The nurse called the woman over. "Myrtle says she doesn't want to put up with your attitude," she told her.

"Oh?" the woman responded. And that was when she started to give me hell. "Is that what she said? Well, she is the one with attitude. I don't know what she's talking about."

I stared at her—this woman was unbelievable. "Do you know what? This is not going to solve anything. We might as well speak to the Director of Care for the facility."

The director was called and as soon as she came down the woman blurted out a lot of things that were untrue. Then she said, "Myrtle is not professional. I'm here to work, not to make friends."

I folded my arms across my chest and fixed her with a cold stare. If she thought she was going to intimidate me, she would have to think again. I turned to the director. "All I want is someone who is willing to work with me," I said. "I don't want to have to deal with her attitude. She's not willing to work with me so I need to be teamed up with someone I can work with."

The woman stepped closer to the director. "Myrtle is unprofessional," she repeated, and then she turned to me, her eyes flashing with anger. "Do you want me to tell the director about you? Don't let me tell the director, you know. I will tell her."

"Why don't you please tell the director my secret?" I said as I glared back at her. I could feel the heat rising in my belly. "Since you seem to have a secret for me please tell the director."

Looking triumphant, she turned to the director. "Myrtle sleeps on the job."

I looked at the nurse in charge, expecting her to intervene and defend me. As the nurse in charge how could she have me sleeping on the job? I was under her supervision, to my surprise, the nurse looked at the director and then at me and said, "Yes, Myrtle, you sleep."

I looked at her, shocked at her declaration. What was she trying to do? The fact was, at some point in time everybody had an incident or two where they fell asleep.

I looked at both women who stood there accusing me and gave them a cold smile. "Tell me something; is this 'tell truth' time?"

They stood there staring at me, not saying anything.

"I want to know if this is 'tell truth' time," I repeated, "because you guys say you are telling the truth. Well, I can tell the truth, too."

I looked at the director. "Both of them sleep." I retorted back to the nurse manager and asked, "How many times have you come into this place and bowed your head at that desk saying you're tired? How many times have you sat there sleeping?" Then I snarled at the other staff member. "And how many times have you gone inside the dining room and put your head down on the table and slept?"

Looking at the director now I said, "Do you know something? We all sleep. The sleeping that they are talking about was after I finished work. The other night, I sat waiting for my shift to end at 11 p.m., so I could swipe out. I sat on a stool inside the TV room—a stool, mind you, not even a chair." I gazed at the other two women, daring them to deny my account. "It was about a quarter to eleven and I dozed off. When these two went through the door it slammed behind them, startling me awake. When I looked at the time it was eleven o'clock. I got up from the stool and watched them walking away down the hallway. You see, that's how they are. They left me sitting there and went on their way."

The Director of Care accepted my explanation, much to the disappointment of my two antagonizers.

At the time of this confrontation, I had only two weeks before I would be transferred to the night shift, away from these two. During those couple of weeks, every time the Director of Care saw me, she would pull me aside. "Myrtle, is everything okay?"

"Yes," I reassured her, "it's okay."

At work I did all that I was supposed to do—I was not about to give anyone the satisfaction of saying I was not fulfilling my duties. Still I was suffering. My body felt weak. At times I would get dizzy spells and would always feel tired. I had to push myself to keep going.

It was time for me to do my annual physical examination—when the results came back I discovered that I was diabetic.

The doctor was very strict with me. She reprimanded me for not exercising and eating correctly; the tears began to flow. When

I left her office that day, I started checking around for another doctor—I even asked my friends for recommendations. I was so distressed. Her response made me feel tremendous guilt about not maintaining my health.

The news hit me hard. I ended up taking a month off work. I thought I was going to die. I went to Jamaica and it was there where I began to come to terms with having diabetes. While in Jamaica I ate a lot of greens, steamed fish, and went jogging. I lost thirteen pounds on that trip. I adjusted my diet, ate properly and began taking medication when I returned to Canada.

I went back to the doctor for my monthly visit to check my results. She was so pleased with my blood-sugar levels and weight loss that she embraced me with a tight hug. She joyfully responded, "Oh, Myrtle, you look so good. I gave you tough love and look at you. I am so proud of you."

Her praise surprised me, as she made me feel as though getting this disease was my fault—I thought she looked down on me after she'd reprimanded me, but I realized she did it only because she cared. I was relieved. I went back to work with a new focus on a healthy lifestyle, I was soon back to normal.

In 2007 I moved my family to a condo. At first we were quite comfortable there, but like many moments in my life it was just the calm before the storm. This time the problem was with our beloved dog, Ashley.

We had only been in the condo a month when Tevin accidentally left the front door open and Ashley ran out into the hallway. Immediately, complaints flooded into the management office.

"You have to get rid of that dog! You're not allowed to have large pets in this building," the manager explained.

Ashley was a little past my knee and quite a bundle of energy. We'd successfully kept her out of sight and out of trouble for one month. Sadly, there was no way around it, she would have to go.

I called my kids and sat them down. "Kids, I'm afraid Ashley won't be able to live with us anymore," I began. "We all love her, but she can't stay in this building anymore."

"Mom, no!" they cried. "We can't give Ashley away."

"I'm sorry, but we can't keep her," I said trying to be firm. As I tried to express the situation, I fought back tears. "We will have to find another home for her."

My children's grieving broke my heart, but I had to stay strong. There was no way that I could get around the rules. I checked around until I found a retired couple who had a home and a lot of love to give. They welcomed Ashley into their loving home. Although parting with our beloved pet was heart-breaking, at least we were comforted by the fact that she would be loved.

I was shocked, when shortly after Ashley's departure her new owners called. They said, "We're so sorry, but we can't keep her. She's so strong and vibrant. We just can't handle a dog like this."

As much as I hated the idea, I ended up taking Ashley to her vet's office. They had a solution, they told me for a monthly fee that Ashley could be kept there until a new home was found. I'd thought this was the answer to our problems, but that was when the real trouble began.

When Ashley left our home a change came over my family. It was as if we had lost a part of ourselves the day our family pet went through the door. The first shock was when Tevin stopped talking.

At fourteen years of age, Tevin was a normal kid. He had a lot of interests, plenty of friends and a full life at school. It all changed when Ashley left. It was as if someone or something had stolen my son's ability to speak. Not a word passed his lips. Paper and pencil became his friends. Each time he needed to say something he ran for a piece of paper to scribble down the words. I had never seen anything like this in all my life.

By this time, Latisha was back at Carleton University where she was enrolled in the pre-law program. I received concerned calls from her friends; informing me that she was not herself. She'd become sad and withdrawn and they could not understand why.

Allicia cried each and every day without fail. Until one day she went to the vet's office to visit her beloved pet. It was as if she could not survive without seeing her, touching her and talking to her. Life was not the same without Ashley.

I started to watch the TV show *Lassie*, I could not get enough of it. There were times when I was late for work because of the television show, *Lassie*. I could not stop watching; it was my connection to Ashley. Each time I watched, I wept.

A week and a half passed and Allicia went to see Ashley on one of her daily visits. One of the kennel workers told her how Ashley cried, hours on end every night. It was so bad that Ashley made all the other dogs' wimper throughout the night as well. When Allicia heard that she said, "I'm taking her for a walk."

Allicia walked her dog all the way home, and then she declared, "Mom, I'm not taking her back. Ashley belongs at home with us."

From that day, family life continued as usual. Tevin started talking again, and Latisha and Allicia were their old selves. I even took a break from watching *Lassie*. But no one was happier to be home than Ashley.

The decision had been made for me. I did not have any other options; I went to the management office and told them I would be selling my condo. I put the property on the market and took all the documents to the office as evidence that I was indeed trying to sell the condo. Only then would they allow me to keep Ashley in the building. It took several months of work by the realtor, but in July of 2008 we moved into our new house further east of the city to the suburb called, Ajax. The house had more than enough room in which to live with Ashley and love her.

In January of 2009, I got bad news. I would have to bury another son of Momma's children—this time it was Uncle Beb. I grew close with him over the years and grew to appreciate his devotion. He was a brute to me when I was growing up, but I knew he didn't know better. Despite all his beatings I knew he loved me. Due to my uncle's upbringing, beatings were his way of guiding and raising me the right way. I've lived to hear my Uncle say, "There's no one like you, and I love the very earth you walk on."

I remember one day Uncle took me aside and said, "Blossom, when I think of all my brothers and sisters and what you've done for me, it's more than they could ever do." As with Aunt Icema's funeral, I took charge of Uncle Beb's ceremony again with some help from other family members, especially Aunt Joyce and my cousin Dell. We made sure that he got a decent funeral.

A few days later I returned to Canada then flew to England to visit family members. I stayed with my cousin, Dell and her husband, Les. I also visited Aunt Winnie, who was now sick and confined to her room. I also met all of her children Dawn, Paul and David.

During my stay in England, I made it my duty to visit Charles and his family. This was my second time visiting Charles, the man who could be my father. By this time, several years later, his children had grown up and most of them had families of their own. He was still tall, handsome and well built. He greeted me with love, respect and humility. His wife greeted me warmly and made sure I was comfortable during my visit with them.

When I was ready to leave, Charles went into his pocket and took out his wallet. Suddenly he was about to hand me some money but my first reaction was to refuse his offer. I explained to him, "All this time I heard that you could be my father, but you have never stretched your hand out to me," I said in a gentle tone. "I don't need the money, but I will take it as a token." With that, I took the money and thanked him, and then we hugged and said our goodbyes.

* * *

Momma's children have aged; some of them are grandparents. Some of them have passed on, and with age, has come a certain level of maturity. I have seen this in my uncles, aunts and now even in my mother.

Now that my mother is older she is just beginning to show me some level of respect and care. The little respect she has to offer is coming much too late. I needed her love and attention when I was a child, when I was a young girl. Now, I am an independent woman.

There was a time when my mother knew in her heart that I would always be there for her no matter what. Regardless of the way she treated me, it was as if she decided that I would be the one taking care of her as she aged. Her expressions of love coming to me now ring hollow as a drum.

In the past it seemed that she was closest to Abraham, her first son. As a child, he used to be sickly, which is probably why she paid a lot of attention to him. She did not get along with Martha, her second daughter. As a result their relationship is still rocky. John her fourth child, was a challenge, she always seemed to have some kind of difficulty with him. Suzette her fifth child withdrew from my mother because of her tendency to make poor decisions, which lead to her being irresponsible. Keith, her last son, curses her whenever and wherever he pleases.

Keith was mother's sixth child. At ten years old, he told the principal at school to F-off. This type of attitude contributed to his disrespectful behaviour. Mother did not reprimand him. Instead she said the principal was jealous of Keith. I turned to her and said, "How could the principal be jealous of Keith, a ten-year old kid?"

"Oh, Keith is smart and he's so bright," she declared. "The principal is jealous."

"Mother," I said, "this principal is in charge of hundreds of kids. What could a ten year old have for a principal to be jealous about?"

When Mother had the chance to mold her young son she let it slip through her fingers. Now it is too late. To this day, Keith has not finished high school and is still struggling to find a job.

Despite our turbulent relationship, I tried reaching out to my mother in later years to cross the chasm between us. After she had moved out of my home, following the accident, we did not maintain much communication. In fact, after not seeing Mother for quite a while, I saw her at my Aunt Icema's funeral in Jamaica. Furthermore, she did not try to talk to me. But I knew that I would be the one to go over and speak with her.

After that I did not see Mother for about four years. A lot had happened between my brother and me. She had the opportunity to say something but she did not. She heard him speak disrespectfully to me and she did not say a word in my defense.

Even in the face of all that, I was always the one who made the first move in an attempt to mend our relationship. I did just that in April 2009, when I began my series of visits to take Mother to places I knew she would enjoy. On one of our early trips, she had thrown on a wig and a pair of pants and I was not happy with the way she looked. It was as if she did not care to put herself together properly to be out with me. For whatever it was worth, she was still my mother and if I was out with her I wanted to be able to say with pride, "This is my mother." She is a beautiful woman, someone who knows how to dress well. However, that day she let herself look less than her best.

I previously asked my brother, Abraham to tell Mother that I was taking her out to dinner and she should get herself dressed. She was living on her own at the time. I was late in getting there and apparently she thought I was not coming again. She was on the balcony looking out and then she saw me and came down. She looked absolutely stunning. She had gone to the hairdresser and was wearing a lovely black dress with cream stripes. It fit snugly at the bust and flared from the waist down. "You look beautiful today," I told her, and I meant it. When we went out, I was pleased; she made me proud in her overall appearance.

I drove Mother to a restaurant in Toronto. When I pulled up, I used the valet parking so that she would not have to walk far; Mother appreciated that. As we got out of the car we enjoyed the beautiful flowers at the entrance.

We enjoyed a wonderful buffet style dinner and afterwards we went to the park. At the end of the evening, Mother thanked me and told me how much she appreciated me taking her out. She enjoyed herself so much and so did I. It was the first connection we ever had together.

\* \* \*

In June 2010, along with several members of the family, I decided to go to a family reunion in Florida. Unfortunately, just before we were about to leave we got the news that Momma's youngest son, Vincent, had passed away. I decided I would head to Jamaica right after the reunion to attend his funeral.

On the way to Florida, we travelled in two cars from Toronto. In one car were Abraham and his wife, and three of their children with Mother. I travelled in the other car with Martha, Allicia, Tevin and two of Martha's children.

Mother and Abraham's wife, Janet had done a lot of cooking that day. "Miss Imo made this for you," Janet said.

Mother said, "Blossom, do you want corn?" Mother piped up and gave me a plate.

"Thanks, I'll have a little," I replied, and sat down to eat.

"You didn't come back to see me," Mother said and to my surprise, she genuinely seemed to have missed me.

We travelled safely to Florida and arrived at our destination. Later that day, we went to the park for our family reunion. There we met Uncle Enos, Uncle Lorenzo and his children Sonia, Andrea, Arlene and Bobby. Aunt Joyce was there with her children Novelette, Ruth, and her twins, Jenny and Janelle. Jenny brought her two children and her husband as well. Novelette was the one who organized this reunion for us along with her mother.

We were all so happy to see one another, especially Mother and her siblings. For me, it was beautiful to see Uncle Lorenzo, Uncle Enos, Aunt Joyce and my mother chatting and reminiscing about old times.

I sat there, taking in the scene, Momma's children talking and laughing together. As I saw the love of these two brothers and two sisters, older now but still a family, a lump rose in my throat and my eyes filled with tears.

*"Oh, Momma, if you could see your children now,"* I cried.

# The Here And Now

# XIX

Sometime ago, Tevin and I lay on my bed talking about the past. I mentioned to him that on October 2, 2010, it had been exactly thirty-four years since I had arrived in Canada.

"Mummy, how did you get here?" he asked.

I told my son that I arrived in Canada with my brothers and sisters. However, because Mother and I could not get along, I decided to go back to Jamaica. Although Jamaica would always be considered my home, at the time I did not see a future for myself there. I explained to Tevin that I wrote to my stepfather and asked if he could assist me in returning to Canada. Upon my arrival back to Canada I explained that his assistance was much appreciated.

The fact was, as a teenager in Kingston my life was rough. I was so naive in a place where people always seemed ready to take advantage of me. Through the help of my mother's husband I am in Canada. Even though he may not always have had the best intentions, he still remained a source of support. He also attempted to help create a relationship between my mother and me. Except, the tragic part with this situation was that my Mother was not looking to build a relationship with me. If it had been up to my mother alone I would never have left Jamaica. Still, I know that on my step-father part he tried.

In truth, for the ten months I spent with my mother in Montreal, I was in hell. Once I moved out, I made it my mission in life to be independent and that is what I did. I lived through many challenges and trials, but I've learned from those mistakes. I have also made progress in this country, which is my second home, and for that I am grateful.

"So, Mom, your stepdad made it possible," Tevin said.

"Yes," I said, without hesitation.

"My grandfather did well," Tevin said.

"Yes," I replied with a small smile, "He helped me to return to Canada and for the kindness he showed me; he did well."

## XX

Over the years, Mother has changed; when she is with me she seems happy. She seems to have mellowed with time, and has even begun to show some affection. Still, I know that if there is any tension between one of her other children and me, she will always take their side.

Mother has never spoken to me about the past. I would love for her to sit down with me and talk about her, me and all that has happened between us. I would love to hear about my father. I wish we could talk about our relationship, why we could not have had a real mother-daughter connection. Still, I have accepted the fact that I will never get that from her.

Sometimes I wonder if it would be easier for my mother to forge a relationship with my children. It seemed that she had an interest once. When the girls were very young, around four and five years old, Mother would bring some lovely dresses for the children. They were so beautiful, I would call them princess dresses because that was what my daughters looked like in them. At that time it seemed that even if she had failed to be a mother to me she would have been a good grandmother to them. I took comfort in that.

Sadly, the strong relationship that I had hoped would blossom never came to be. When Allicia had the accident, Mother became so emotional when anyone would talk would about it around her. It would be so stressful for her. It seemed she could not bear to think about her granddaughter suffering. As soon as anyone began to say something about the accident she would whisper, "No, don't tell me. Don't tell me." Each time she would see Allicia she would display great attention.

Mother has not been as close to my children as I would have wished. Sometimes a simple phone call is all it would take. I regret that, even with this second chance, it is as if a close relationship with my mother was not meant to be.

Although I witness the joy of my mother when I take her out, unsettling memories keep me from moving on completely. I am still an orphan at heart and I am still without the love of a mother or father.

I am a woman, I am a mother, and I am an independent person. Yes, I am all that. But still, I was also a child. I am that child who still yearns for a mother's soft touch, gentle words, warm hugs, and the knowledge of knowing that you are loved. I am still the child who seeks connection with her roots, her father, and her bloodline. I am the child who wants to hear from her mother's lips, "Blossom, you make me proud."

When I think of my life and how I have reached out my hand to assist others, my mother's appreciation was not there. This brings back memories of the treatment I received from her; and the tears are quick to flow. Seeking my mother, "Dearest'" love does not matter to me anymore at this point and time in my life. Still I wish her all the best.

*Where are you now, my mother?*

# XXI

As I reflect on my life, I realize that I have overcome so many obstacles. Some would say more than my fair share, but still I hold my head high and keep looking forward.

As a child I grew up not knowing who my father was. Although there were two possibilities I never enjoyed a real father-daughter relationship with either one of these gentlemen. I would have loved to have had a father visiting me, to play with me, and to give me advice. But that was not meant to be, it will forever be a mystery.

The name my mother gave me began to comprise meaning. As I transitioned into adulthood, my name is something I still resent; however, it has become a part of me. I acknowledge and accept who I am today and changing my name would mean changing who I am and who I am destined to be.

As a young woman I suffered sexual molestation, a narrow escape from rape, a failed marriage and domestic abuse. My yearning for a relationship with a parent, whether mother or father never materialize. Would I be blessed instead with a loving, caring relationship with a spouse? Unfortunately, my relationships did not last. Were they not meant to be?

As a woman I struggled to raise a family on my own. It was hard being both mother and father to my children. It was hard, trying to meet the financial needs of three growing children. But I was a fighter. I had been through many trials and I had never let them swallow me up. I was not going to give up now.

Later on in life my family and I suffered a traumatic accident, one that almost robbed me of my beloved children. One in which my daughter was left clinging to life, and also left my mother severely injured. It has taken years for us to gradually recover and begin to live a normal life again. For my daughter, Allicia, it has been years of struggle, work and determination. She has grown into a beautiful young woman and I thank God that was meant to be.

And so I give thanks.

From my relationships, even though they did not last forever as I would have hoped, I have three wonderful children whom I love dearly. They are the bright lights in my life, a source of great happiness.

So as I reflect on my life, on my past, and on my struggles, I will not dwell on what was not meant to be.

Instead I give praises for what I have.

# EPILOGUE

What is love? From childhood until now I have craved that elusive thing which is called love. My grandmother gave me all she had, but still I yearned for more. I wanted my mother to love me. I wanted a father to love me. I wanted to find true love in my relationships. But did I ever find these mysterious things that I sought for?

At this point in my life I am grateful. I have a family of three beautiful children. Though my family and I faced trauma, pain and fear, we overcame it all. Last summer Allicia graduated from college with a diploma in Tourism, Management, Culture and Heritage. In addition to her completion of a diploma, she is going to pursue another diploma in Community and Justice Service. After seeing the determination and tenacity that she displayed since her accident, I have no doubt that one day she will achieve her dreams.

Latisha is pursuing a dream of her own. She has completed her Bachelors in Public Affairs at Carleton University in Ottawa, with graduation scheduled for 2012. As she prepares for her entrance examinations for law school, she can see that her goal of becoming a lawyer is within reach. She will not let anything sway her from the career she has chosen.

My last child, Tevin who has successfully completed high school, has proven to be a wizard in the kitchen. He has dreams of becoming a world-class chef and his heart is set on pursuing the culinary arts program at college. Tevin knows where he wants to go in life and I will do everything in my power to help him get there.

I am proud of my children, their achievements, ambitions and their dreams. They are my greatest blessing in life.

The joy I feel when I can bring happiness to others is very enlightening. Even as my heart melted with sadness, one of my happiest moments was when I was able to fulfill Momma's ultimate dream, to see Minister Powell in the pulpit one last time. Another happy time for me was when I was there for Aunt Icema at a time when she needed me. It also filled me with joy when I was able to help Uncle Beb live comfortably in his last years.

I still wish for the strong arms of a father to surround me. But in the midst of my longing, I have resolved to find true happiness by helping others. This is the way I have been able to find joy.

For those who wonder why I have written this book, it is my way of releasing the pain that has been pent up inside me all these years. It is also my way of sharing my story with the world. Through this story, I hope to help others. I have been through a lot, but my story is one that I hope will inspire others to be strong, to never give up.

This, my story, is the way I will heal, the way I will forgive, the way I will love.

*Mother, Dearest, I am free!!!*

*Free Indeed!*

# ABOUT THE AUTHOR

Myrtle Morrison continues to dedicate her life to her children, and to helping others, particularly the elderly for whom she has a special love. Myrtle lives with her children and faithful pet, Ashley, in Ajax (Ontario, Canada). Myrtle is still in search of love and fulfillment, but remains optimistic about her future endavours.

*"We the abused never forget. Certain memories will remain in our thoughts forever. Memories of the past are something we should never hold inside, but rather talk about it with someone we trust. Saying goes you can forgive but not forget.*

*To the abuser, you know who you are. You probably will forget or have forgotten because you are obviously not the victim, but remember this "whatever is done in darkness shall come to light".*